WORTHY OF LOVE

Other Books by Debbie Mirza

The Narcissism Series – Book One

The Covert Passive Aggressive Narcissist:
Recognizing the Traits and Finding Healing
After Hidden Emotional and Psychological Abuse

The most common description a survivor of this type of relationship will use is crazy-making. The emotional abuse and gaslighting makes you question your own view of reality, and sometimes your own sanity. You will know after reading this book if the person you are with is a covert narcissist, and your experience with them will begin to make sense for the first time.

The Safest Place Possible: A Guide to Healing and Transformation

This book is a journey of healing through self-love.

It is both a memoir and a gentle guide for your own transformation. You will learn 21 simple, yet powerful self-love exercises.

If you have lost yourself in an unhealthy relationship and want to find your way back to who you really are, if you are experiencing anxiety and fear, if you are unsure of your future, this is the book for you.

The Safest Place Possible: Companion Workbook

This workbook is the companion to Debbie's book, *The Safest Place Possible*. It will help you apply the 21 life-changing exercises the author uses in her own life as well as with her clients to help you transform the relationship you have with yourself. It is also great for book clubs and support groups.

Praise for Worthy of Love

To say my professional world was rocked when I read Debbie Mirza's *The Covert Passive Aggressive Narcissist* is only a mild exaggeration. After all, as a decades-long psychotherapist, I thought I knew pretty much what there was to know about narcissism. How wrong I was. In that book, Debbie did nothing short of expanding the clinical, "textbook" understanding of narcissism—introducing entirely new ways to think about narcissists and how we identify them.

Lucky for us, Debbie Mirza has done it again with *Worthy of Love*. And thank goodness! With her trademark generous spirit, she allows us a window into her own painful experience and recovery journey. The confusion, the strange physical ailments, the sheer breakdown of self that comes part and parcel with narcissistic relationships. All real. But what do we do with all of it? How do we heal?

Worthy of Love spells out the steps Debbie took to heal herself. She stresses the need for deprogramming and rebuilding after narcissistic abuse and she shares with you, dear reader, just how to get that done. Debbie asks the hard questions—she even provides space for you to answer them!—while gently guiding you toward fully loving and trusting yourself again after narcissistic abuse.

Perhaps most importantly, Debbie reminds us we are not crazy, and we are not alone in this. We can find our way back to wholeness and peace. You may be starting this process from a place of emotional chaos, thinking you may never recover your peace of mind or return to your old self. Fear not. With Debbie at the helm, you're in the most capable of hands.

— Abby Rodman, Psychotherapist and
Co-Host of the *Sisters Cracking Up* podcast

As a mental health professional working with survivors of abusive relationships, I am always looking for tools to assist in the journey of healing. Debbie Mirza has given us an invaluable resource with this book. *Worthy of Love* is a compassionate guidebook packed full of insight and practical advice. Included are healing exercises designed to allow the reader space to reflect on their own experience. Debbie addresses questions which tend to haunt survivors, such as:

"How did I let myself be treated this way?"
"Will I ever feel like myself again?"
"How do I know who to trust?"

She shares parts of her own story and in doing so, offers hope for a life of resilience and joy to survivors who are caught in the confusion and pain of recovering from toxic relationships. Debbie's gentle approach gives the reader the sense of a wise, supportive friend who is walking with them step by step on their path toward wholeness. This offering from Debbie Mirza will be a staple in my personal library and a recommendation for any of my clients seeking to rebuild their lives and trust themselves again.

— Elizabeth Brekelbaum,
Licensed Professional Counselor

In 2018, I was working hard to both understand, and then to heal, from a thirty-year-long experience that I simply could not comprehend at that point.

A friend had said that some of what I had experienced sounded more than a little narcissistic. Having no real knowledge or understanding of narcissism I embarked on a journey of learning via books, research, and more YouTube videos than I care to remember. There was one, though, that would change my life.

I had been following Meredith Miller's work and so watched each of her videos as she uploaded them. Of all of them, the one that really caught my eye was where she was interviewing a woman who had just written a book. I found myself watching it with increasing intensity as the discussion outlined so many things I hadn't heard anywhere else. I was also drawn to the authenticity of both of these women. It screamed out to me that these two people not only really 'got it,' but they had clearly 'been there' too. I watched the video several more times before ordering the book that was to be the catalyst of change for me, *The Covert Passive Aggressive Narcissist* by Debbie Mirza.

The book was a revelation to me, so beautifully written and full of content that resonated so well. I read it in a day and reread it repeatedly over the coming weeks. I remember excitedly taking it to my next therapy session and saying to Clare, my Dr. of Counselling Psychology, 'This is it! This woman really gets it!' I had finally found something that made sense of what had happened to me.

As relieved as it felt to have found this book, I was equally shocked and horrified at the stark realisation that this was the truth of my situation. I realised almost immediately that for me, there could not be the thorough healing I so desperately sought without deep and comprehensive understanding, and so I committed to researching covert narcissism to find further answers. This required my reaching out to Debbie, and to my surprise and unceasing gratitude, she replied.

I couldn't have possibly known when I first reached out to her that I would be calling her my 'partner in healing' within just a few short years. I am privileged, honoured, and blessed to now be able to call Debbie my friend and colleague. I am sincerely thankful for the love, support, and wisdom she has brought to me. It has been lifechanging and something for which I will be forever grateful.

Our friendship blossomed as we ended up working together in Debbie's online support group, which I am honoured to be the lead admin of.

In the following pages, Debbie brings her own personal experiences—and the learning she has derived from them—to life. Her work to overcome the issues in her own life that so many of us also face, are revealed here, through easy-to-use processes that address the very real emotional, psychological, and physiological issues that we so often find ourselves struggling with.

Debbie both recognises and offers support and strategies in the following pages to help those affected by narcissistic abuse. She has once again stepped forward to help fill the void of support, help, learning, and validation in providing yet another safe space here to explore and come to better understand ourselves, our relationships, and our situations.

Throughout the book, Debbie has included both time and physical space for each reader to pause and reflect on their own experiences/relational dynamics at various points along the way. This is an invaluable tool and is no doubt something that will be returned to and built upon throughout each reader's healing journey.

You are in safe, kind, experienced, and compassionate hands here. May they hold you and support you well as you turn each page and embrace the challenge of actively working toward a happier, healthier future that you so deserve.

> Much love to you all,
> LINDA BARNES
> Creator of the *Is it Me?* Podcast Series on Spotify
> Lead Admin for Debbie Mirza's Online Support Group
> Manchester, U.K.

~

Worthy
of Love

Reclaiming the Truth of Who You Are

A GENTLE AND RESTORATIVE PATH TO HEALING AFTER NARCISSISTIC ABUSE

Debbie Mirza

SAFE PLACE PUBLISHING

Worthy of Love –A Gentle and Restorative Path
to Healing After Narcissistic Abuse

by Debbie Mirza

© 2021 Debbie Mirza
Published by Safe Place Publishing, Monument, CO

For permission requests, write to the author, addressed:

Attention Permissions Coordinator at
DebbieMirzaAuthor@gmail.com

Editor: Kelly Madrone
Proofreader: Michelle Morgan
Book designer: BookSavvyStudio.com

Library of Congress Control Number: 2021923520
ISBN: 978-0-9986213-8-8 (paperback)
ISBN: 978-0-9986213-9-5 (ebook)
First Edition
Printed in the United States of America

～

Note to Reader: This publication is meant as a source of valuable information for the reader, however it is not meant as a substitute for direct expert assistance. The author is not a licensed mental health professional and her advice is not intended as a substitute for consultation with a licensed practitioner. If such level of assistance is required, the services of a competent professional should be sought.

DEDICATION

To all those who have experienced narcissistic abuse.
May you always know how amazing you are, how strong, how
brave, and how beautiful you are. May you always feel cherished,
valued, and loved. You deserve everything your heart longs for.

Contents

Acknowledgements..xiii

Foreword - Bree Bonchay, LCSW...................................... xvii

Introduction xix

1. The Discard: The Beginning of My Awakening...................1

2. Anger, Depression, and Complex PTSD........................ 9

3. Running Away and Learning
   How to Take Care of My Heart 17

4. A Deeper Layer of Healing 27

5. Relentless Attacks and the Rise of a
   Life-Changing Decision 35

6. Learning the Balance of Giving and Receiving............. 39

7. Learning to Trust My Own Guidance
   as My Health Fell Apart..47

8. Trauma and the Nervous System 55

9. Did They Ever Really Love You? 67

10. Forgiving Yourself for Not Seeing 71

11. Why Narcissists Behave the Way They Do...................73

12. Why Many Survivors Wonder if They are the Narcissist 81

13. Why Do We End Up with Narcissists? 85

14. Dating Again 89

15. Smear Campaigns and Flying Monkeys..................... 95

16. Rewriting Destructive Messages 99

17. Learning to Trust Yourself 115

18. Boundaries...119

19. Relearning What Love Looks Like through
    Self-Care and Self-Love 127

20. The In-Between 129

21. The Perks of Being on Your Own 131

22. Relearning Who You Are 137

23. Where I Am Now with My Healing 145

24. This is Your Hero's Journey.. 153

25. Designing Your New Life 157

26. A Love Letter 161

Resources...163

About the Author...165

Acknowledgements

To MY MOM. THANK YOU FOR GIVING ME A FOUNDATION of unconditional love, the greatest gift you could have ever given me. You were an angel on Earth, and I was so lucky to be your daughter. I will forever hold you in my heart, beautiful soul.

To my dad. Thank you for taking care of Mom so well when she was going through dementia, for all those years, up until the very end when we had to say goodbye. You are a special man. I treasure the closeness we have had in recent years. Thank you for loving me. Thank you for your generous heart. Your consistent presence in my life is a gift that I will cherish forever.

To my sister, Sonia. You hold a special place in my heart. Your tender heart and wealth of wisdom have been there for me so many times throughout the years, and I am so grateful for you. We have been through so much together and have a bond that only sisters can have. I cherish you beyond words. Thank you for loving me. Thank you for being there for me and reminding me who I was during the times I felt so lost and unclear. You were a lifeline for me during my lowest times. Thank you, beautiful Sonia. I love you so much and I feel incredibly blessed to have you as my sister.

To Cassie. Where do I begin... Tears begin falling as I write your name. I love you so incredibly much. To have watched you grow from the first moment you took a breath until now is one of the greatest privileges I have had in this life. You are such a special soul. You light up my world, and anyone else who gets to be around you. You bring color, clarity, and adventure to my life, and I cherish every moment I get to have with you. You are so creative, so wise, so strong. You are your own person and I learn so much from you. Thank you for being in my life. I am so honored and lucky to have you as my daughter. Thank you for who you are. Always know that you are incredibly cherished and worthy of everything your heart desires.

To Curtis. I am so lucky and blessed to have a son like you. You are amazing. I learn so much from you and feel so lucky and blessed to be your mom. Your heart and your mind are so special. Thank you for your kindness, your honesty, and for always being fully yourself. Thank you for your humor. You and Cassie make me laugh like no one else. I love hearing your perspective on things. I love our deep talks and our fun ones. I hope you always know you are perfect just the way you are. May you always have the courage to be fully you. May you always live your life on your terms and love the life you create. I can't wait to see how you choose to express the brilliance inside you.

To Liz. My heart. My queen. My best friend in the whole wide world. Oh boy. Here come the tears. Liz, you have been my steadfast friend for so many years. I loved you from the moment I met you in seventh grade. In all that time I have never once felt judged by you. I have only and always felt love and complete acceptance. As soon as I hear your voice, I feel like I can exhale. I feel so absolutely safe with you. There is no way I can put into words how much you mean to me. I wish everyone in the world could have a best friend like you. You are love personified. Anyone who gets to be in your presence is incredibly lucky. You light up the world, Liz, and I feel lucky and blessed to have you as my best friend. We have walked each other through so many stages of life, and I have always felt completely free to be myself with you. There is no greater gift anyone could ever give me. Thank you. Thank you. Thank you. I love you, my friend.

To Sonja. I love you so much! From the moment we met I knew we would be lifelong friends. You are like no one else I know, and you see aspects of me that no one else sees. I will be forever grateful for your presence in my life, and for our friendship. I have so many unique and special memories with you. Sitting in a treehouse overlooking a river in silence and feeling such peace and freedom to just be there in the moment with you. Magical experiences in the

Louvre and Saint-Sulpice. Feeling off-the-charts excitement and joy with you walking through the Moroccan store in Ashland. Thank you for being you. Thank you for loving me and seeing me. I cherish our friendship so much.

To Noura. I adore you. You are such a special spirit and light. You live to the beat of your own drum, and I absolutely love it! I love the ease I feel with you when we talk and spend time together. You are a breath of fresh air and I appreciate you so much! Thank you for being uniquely you. Thank you for always being so honest and having a heart that is so available and tender. You have a strength and steadiness about you that is so comforting. What you bring to this world, Noura, is incredibly special. Thank you for being my friend. You hold a special place in my heart.

To Linda. You are such a gift and a treasure. I would not have been able to run the support group without you. Thank you for being a steadfast support and friend to me. Your wisdom and protective nature are invaluable and mean so much. I am so grateful for your friendship, chuckie, and for introducing me to the term chuckie. Someday we will meet in person, and I can't wait! Thank you for being you. You are so special. The world is lucky to have you, and I am too.

To my cousins from South Africa. You are like brothers and sisters to me. You have been a consistent presence in my life of love and kindness, and I cherish and value each one of you, and every moment I get to spend with you. Thank you for your humor, your music, your genuineness, and all the memories we have shared. I love you all so very much.

To the members of my support group. Thank you for letting me be a part of your lives. Thank you for your courage to be vulnerable, and your profound strength to survive what you have. You are so brave, and I am honored to be a part of your important healing journey.

To Kelly Madrone. Thank you so much for the wonderful work you do. I always learn so much from your notes and edits. You are a pleasure to work with, and I am so grateful for you! You are an editor extraordinaire!

To Michelle Morgan. Thank you for proofreading this manuscript! You are always a joy to work with. I love your colorful and helpful notes. They make me smile and educate me at the same time. So grateful for you.

To Chris Mole. I am so glad we met in Ashland! Just before "the doors closed"! You are multitalented and I am so grateful for you! You are such a pleasure to work with. Your gentle energy and creative insights helped bring ease, flow, and joy to this process. Thank you so much for all you did!

Foreword

BY Bree Bonchay, LCSW

FOR MANY NARCISSISTIC ABUSE SURVIVORS, the end of an abusive relationship does not mean that there is also an immediate end to the emotional and psychological pain caused by these damaging relationships. The effects of narcissistic abuse can have a lasting impact and wreak havoc on a survivor's mental and physical health if left unmanaged.

The reality is many survivors will go on to experience symptoms of a trauma disorder or meet the Diagnostic and Statistical Manual of Mental Disorders, Fifth Edition (DSM-V) criteria for post-traumatic stress disorder in the aftermath of an abusive relationship, requiring professional treatment and intervention. Exposure to chronic psychological and/or physical abuse often makes the abuse survivor begin to doubt their judgment and ability to take care of themselves. Abuse can warp their self-image, even making them believe they deserved the abuse or that they are the abuser. Sadly, survivors often feel paralyzed and helpless to take the necessary steps to relieve their suffering and seek professional help.

This is why it's appalling that there is not more concern and resources for survivors, and it's equally appalling that there is not more preventative education about the individuals who perpetrate this abuse and have some of the most dangerous disorders in the DSM-V, such as psychopathy, antisocial personality disorder, and narcissistic personality disorder.

I have been a psychotherapist for over 20 years, but it was not until 2014 that the overwhelming need for public education and survivor resources came to my attention, and I began sharing my insights about the impact of these dangerous disorders in interpersonal relationships. In response to the lack of public awareness about this form of abuse, in 2016, I created World Narcissistic Abuse Awareness Day, which is recognized every first of June. Then in 2017, I launched the first global summit on the topic with the dual mission of providing much-needed public education and healing resources for recovery to survivors around the globe.

Since I began my work in this new genre of psychology, I have been fortunate to get the opportunity to meet and interview many experts on the topic. One of them was Debbie Mirza.

I quickly learned that Debbie has the lovely ability to be able to convey her knowledge with the warmth of a trusted friend and with the hard-earned wisdom of someone who bears the scars of the trials only a survivor of narcissistic abuse can fully understand. And, most particularly, in her book, *Worthy of Love*, she offers you the hope and assurance that understands that although recovery is not going to be easy, you don't have to navigate this uncharted territory alone. You get to join Debbie as she guides you along the path she has forged, always knowing that she believes you are worthy of love and capable of overcoming the trauma of narcissistic abuse, even if you aren't able to believe it right now.

> — Bree Bonchay, LCSW
> Founder of the World Narcissistic Abuse
> Awareness Day Summits, and Author of
> *I Am Free: Healing Stories about Surviving
> Relationships with Narcissists and Sociopaths*

Introduction

"IS IT EVEN POSSIBLE TO HEAL AFTER THESE RELATIONSHIPS?" one woman in our support group asked. This is a real and understandable question for someone who has experienced narcissistic abuse.

This type of emotional and psychological abuse affects so many areas of a survivor's life. Your very life-force energy diminishes over time. After so much gaslighting, you lose a clear sense of who you are. Your self-esteem and self-worth can feel nonexistent because of ongoing devaluing and demeaning behavior.

Your physical body is affected as well. Many survivors have health issues, often chronic conditions that affect how they are able to live and function in the world.

It is common to have symptoms of Complex PTSD, such as reliving traumatic experiences through flashbacks, feeling like you live in a continual state of high alert, being jumpy and sensitive to stimuli, having difficulty sleeping, feeling toxic guilt and shame, experiencing a lack of emotional regulation, and feeling like you are permanently damaged or worthless.

Cognitive dissonance wreaks havoc on your mind and body as you try to make sense of what you have been through and get clear on the truth about the person you love and thought loved you.

Many find themselves becoming more reclusive after these relationships, feeling a new distrust of others and the world around them.

This type of abuse can take you to depths of despair that make you wonder if you will ever be able to recover.

I have personally been to those depths in my own life. I have experienced everything I mentioned above and more, as I am sure many of you have. I know this pain and confusion well.

Over the past several years, since I first learned about covert narcissism and began to unravel what I had been through, I have done a lot of healing work on myself, and I am here to tell you there is a light at the end of this tunnel, and healing is possible.

In my book, *The Covert Passive Aggressive Narcissist*, I included a chapter on healing. I have learned so much more about the healing process since writing that book, I felt I needed and wanted to share with you all I have learned since then.

This book will begin with my own story of healing. I have decided to share what my path of healing looked like because hearing what others have gone through in story form helps us heal as well. It helps validate our own experience, while also letting us know we are not alone. Our circumstances may be different, but the essence of what we experience after being in relationships with people with narcissistic personality disorder (NPD) have many commonalities.

Those of us who have experienced such abuse often feel alone in it, because unless someone has gone through it, there is no way they can fully understand. So it is both helpful and healing to hear or read someone else's story.

I also want to share my personal journey because I want to give you hope. I have discovered a lot in my healing process and have come out of the dark times and I want you to know and see there is life on the other side of this.

You will be a witness to the arc of my evolution and transformation. You will see the change in me over time and read about the things I did that made a profound impact on my healing.

Toward the end of the book, I will share in more detail where I am with my healing at this point in my life.

I will also explain three stages of healing that are common among survivors. I will address recurring questions that come up after we have realized we have been with a narcissist. You will read about situations that often arise after leaving a narcissist, as well as how to deal with them.

I will share essential elements I believe are necessary and profoundly helpful to heal and fully recover. I will also lead you through several writing exercises that will help you rewrite the false messages you have received from narcissists as well as heal other damaging effects.

I will explain ways to safeguard yourself from ever getting in these relationships again.

We'll cover all these topics and more. Then we will look ahead to the new life you are building and the new way of being you are developing. You will find out why I refer to this healing path as your hero's journey.

You have been through an extraordinary amount, and you deserve to heal.

The fact that you picked up this book tells me you are a special kind of human, and I am so happy you are here. To have experienced what you have and pursue healing after it reveals a lot about you, and I hope you are already incredibly proud of yourself for taking steps to heal your tender and important heart.

You deserve to see, feel, and know the truth of your magnificence.

Your life and light will return, and you will experience living in a very different way. You will become that safe, trusted place you long for. You will feel the exhale you desire. And the power you once gave away to others will return to its rightful and deserving owner—you.

CHAPTER ONE

The Discard: The Beginning
of My Awakening

HAVE HAD SEVERAL NARCISSISTS IN MY LIFE. They have been relatives, friends, romantic partners, and colleagues. Some of these relationships have lasted a couple years, and others for decades. All of them have been the covert type, the most difficult form of narcissism to recognize. This is why many continued for so long—I was not able to see the subtle emotional and psychological abuse.

It was a long-term romantic relationship that became the catalyst for my awakening to the realization and understanding of covert narcissism, along with the damaging effects these relationships have had on me throughout my life.

My awakening began in the wake of the discard phase of this relationship.

As I tell my story, I won't be sharing the details of this relationship or others, for my own protection. The focus will be on my personal healing path. We have put our focus and attention on the narcissists for way too long anyway, wouldn't you agree? It's our turn now. It's our turn to focus on ourselves, our own healing and realization of the beautiful truth of our own magnificence and restorative ability.

I have found with my own healing and in talking with others who have experienced narcissistic abuse that there seem to be three common phases, or stages, we go through as we heal. The first one is the Realization and Education stage, followed by a Cocooning phase, which we enter as a result of a buildup of overwhelm after prolonged and ongoing trauma. As we become stronger and clearer, we enter the Dreaming and Rebuilding stage.

The Realization and Education stage begins when we first discover we have been with a narcissist. Typically we begin our awakening with a tremendous amount of research on narcissism. Often we turn to research when we're experiencing heightened abuse or after we've been discarded by the narcissist (and sometimes this heightened abuse occurs as part of the discard phase). If this is a divorce or breakup, we experience the challenge of making big life decisions while being gaslighted, controlled, and demeaned more than ever, as the abuse intensifies. This is an unsettling, confusing, crazy-making, and incredibly painful time, but it will become the foundation for ultimate healing and freedom. The information we receive at this time is crucial for us to learn so we can understand what we have been experiencing and begin to work through the cognitive dissonance.

After this time of extreme upheaval in our lives, and having endured prolonged and ongoing abuse, many of us reach a place of burnout. We are emotionally and physically exhausted from so much emotional and psychological abuse. We have experienced so much shock and confusion at the other person's behavior, and are feeling the gravity of all we went through during the years before the discard. Our world feels like it is too much to bear, and for many of us, during the Cocooning phase we understandably retreat inward.

This is also a necessary and important stage. We make our world smaller. We stay home more. We only talk to a few people we really trust. We need quiet. We long for stillness and calm. We need things to settle down inside us and around us. We often feel deep sadness and grief during this time, and many of us feel alone. This can be mixed with feelings of relief from not having to live with the narcissist anymore or having them so involved in our lives. It is during this time that great healing can come about. This is a time to be gentle and kind with ourselves. Our heart is wounded, and it needs care and attention. Our body is weathered, worn, and needs to slow down. We need to know and feel we are safe, and that everything is going to be okay.

As we gradually and gently emerge from this stage, the world begins to open up for us. We begin to feel like entering back into life. We still experience some flashbacks, anxiety, sadness, anger, and fear, but now we have learned and are continuing to learn how to be with ourselves there. There is still some deprogramming to do from the cult-like experience we left, but inside us things are settling down. We find ourselves beginning to dream again. This is when we begin to enter the third stage of Dreaming and Rebuilding.

We have been beaten down in so many ways for so long. We have learned a lot and taken time to slow down and take care ourselves, and now we are ready to work on creating a life that feels wonderful. We see more how worthy and deserving we are of a beautiful life, and we have hope that we might be able to enjoy life going forward.

You will see these three phases play out in my story. There is a linear sequence to these, as well as some overlap. There have been different times in my journey where I have needed to cocoon again, and times where I sought more education to understand another aspect of narcissism I was experiencing. I am in the third stage right now in my life, and it feels amazing. I feel free.

My Realization and Education stage began during the breakup of the long-term romantic relationship I mentioned earlier. This phase of my healing story began when someone told me the person I was with sounded like a narcissist.

I was shocked to hear that word associated with this person, but when she explained the classic traits she was seeing, I became intrigued and knew I needed to look into this more. There was no doubt I was experiencing confusing and crazy-making behavior, and I needed to figure out what was happening. On my way home I stopped at a bookstore and began researching narcissism.

Most of what I read was a description of an overt narcissist—a person who is flashy, showy, obnoxious, obviously self-centered, and full of themselves. At first, I wondered if I was on the wrong track because some of what I read did not fully describe what I was experiencing. At the same time, there were many things that rang true.

When I got home, I searched the internet, watched videos, and read articles on the topic of narcissism. The more I learned, the more it seemed I was on the right track, but I still felt confused because I wasn't finding anything that fully described my situation.

I decided to reach out to life coaches in an online community I was a part of. I posted the question, "Are there any coaches in this group who know about narcissism?" I heard back from one and made an appointment with her immediately. In our session she asked me questions such as, "What were your birthdays like?"

"That's interesting you ask that," I said, "because I've never been able to figure out why I end up in tears on most of my birthdays, why I dread them now, and why I feel depleted of energy by the end of the day."

"That's very common," she responded. She then explained how narcissists sabotage birthdays, holidays, and any days that are special or important to you.

The conversation was eye-opening, but still I wondered if I was reading into things or being dramatic, trying to find fault where perhaps there wasn't any. My confusion was a result of the gaslighting I was experiencing and my cognitive dissonance at the time, but I continued my search because I had seen and heard enough things that lined up.

After months of researching, I found another coach who knew about narcissism. In our conversation she said something that made everything come together for me.

I took the first 45 minutes of the hour-long session to tell her about this relationship and answer any questions she had. When I was done, she said the words I needed to hear, offering the missing piece to this confusing puzzle. "This person you've been with sounds like a covert passive-aggressive narcissist, and they are the most difficult type to recognize." My jaw dropped open and the hairs on my arms stood on end. I felt the chills of truth. Until that moment, I had not heard of this type of narcissism. This gave me new words to begin searching and with them, I was able to piece together more and more information that began to help me make sense of all I had experienced in the relationship.

I continued to talk to therapists and coaches, and later joined a local support group for narcissistic abuse, where I flooded the room with as many questions as I could possibly ask. I was a sponge for any helpful information I could get. For the first time, things were beginning to come together and make sense. Feelings I had felt for so long were being validated.

Even though the pieces were coming together for me intellectually, my heart was still enduring a tremendous amount of suffering. I was being treated in ways that were shocking, disturbing, and incredibly painful.

My self-esteem was at an all-time low. I had lived for so long with subtle demeaning messages about myself and devaluing behavior. I wondered if what I was told, and what had been implied to me about myself, actually was true. I wasn't able to see myself clearly at the time and had learned to believe others more than myself. Maybe I really was lazy. Maybe I was a drain and expected others to take care of me. Maybe I was entitled, and self-sabotaged, was too dramatic, too sensitive, too opinionated, too stubborn, annoying, not considerate, selfish, materialistic, bad with friendships, not open to other people's advice, undisciplined, not appreciative, controlling, manipulative, too rigid, didn't take responsibility for myself, disappointing, hard to live with, too much, not enough, and definitely not worthy of love, kindness, and respect. And above all, maybe it was true that I was unlovable, and that the only way for me to become lovable was if I changed who I was.

These messages I had received for so long played in my mind often. I was unsure of what the truth was because I felt like I couldn't see myself clearly. I figured someone who lived with me would know me well, so what I was hearing must be accurate. I wondered if I just couldn't see the truth about myself. I would call my best friend and my sister and ask them what they saw in me. They had known me longer than the person I was with, so I trusted their views, which were totally opposite of these negative memes. But then I would think, *Maybe they are just being nice. They don't live with me, so maybe they don't see the unpleasant and unlikable sides of me.*

I am at a place now where I clearly see that these negative and destructive messages are not true, but instead are a reflection of someone else's unresolved issues. People who are cruel, people who are bullies, have very low self-esteem and a lot of hidden hatred toward themselves. The covert types are tricky because they appear so put-together, confident, and articulate. They turn things around on us—the targets—so we don't notice the truth about them. It is a way of gaslighting, manipulating, and controlling.

It is important to know that we treat others the way we treat ourselves. When we feel love and acceptance of self and tenderness inside, we naturally give those messages to people around us. They feel loved, they feel lifted and energized, not drained. So, when narcissists, who are essentially bullies, give us negative messages about ourselves, it reflects what is going on inside *them*, and ultimately has nothing to do with who *we* are.

At the time, I could not see this.

In addition to my low self-worth, I had very little belief in myself when it came to handling life on my own. That is another effect of being with a narcissist. They often create a dependence on them that makes us feel as if we are incapable of living life without them.

I was traumatized daily. I felt small, powerless, and afraid. I felt alone.

I was in a state of disbelief and utter confusion.

Also, as a result of the discard, I had to deal with many logistical concerns. This was especially difficult because at that time I was struggling to make decisions.

Most mornings I didn't want to get out of bed. I woke up sobbing and went to bed in the same condition. I was an emotional wreck.

After the relationship officially ended, I moved to a different city and rented a home closer to my dad. The discard was over and I felt relief at not having toxic energy around me anymore.

CHAPTER TWO

Anger, Depression, and Complex PTSD

E VEN THOUGH THE DISCARD WAS PAINFUL, there were so many things I enjoyed about being in a different home and being single. I loved being able to make decisions on my own. I loved not having to check in with anyone else. I loved having my bedroom all to myself, to only feel my energy at nighttime. I loved the quiet. The stillness. The freedom to let my feelings out.

As my body was able to relax a bit more in this new quiet space, I felt more freedom to feel all the emotions I had not felt safe to fully feel and let out before.

As the emotions came to the surface, I felt angry. So angry at the way I had been treated. Angry at the cruelty I had experienced. And shock. I was stunned and confused at the behavior I had witnessed and received. It was especially disorienting because what I experienced during the discard phase was nothing like what I had experienced during most of the relationship. As with most covert narcissists, during the discard phase the classic traits of NPD become more pronounced, more overt. The narcissist's behavior becomes more callous and cold. Their rage is more pronounced. The emotional and psychological attacks become relentless. And when they are done with you, you feel kicked to the curb, thrown out, and easily replaced.

The truth is, this behavior had always been there, it was just more hidden. My body and heart had felt it at a subconscious level. I was feeling the repercussions of years of hidden abuse, coupled with the overt abuse that emerged. Emotions I had held inside me for a long time now felt more free, more safe to come out.

I felt grief. Deep grief. I had endured so much for so long, and I had changed as a result. I almost didn't recognize the woman I was.

I used to have so much life in me. So much zest for life. I was a dreamer, an eternal optimist. I was open, outgoing, a people person. My inner essence was vibrant. I am someone who gets excited about the smallest things. There is a light in me that no matter how much I get knocked down seems to always come back. But now, that light was greatly diminished.

During this time I did a lot of reflecting on the relationship, noticing things I hadn't seen before. I would replay confusing conversations in my mind. I journaled a lot, trying to make sense of what I had been through and was still going through. It helped to write things down. Things were becoming more and more clear to me even though the cognitive dissonance was still strong. When you see someone a certain way for so long, it's difficult to accept the truth of who they are, and in fact, who they have been the whole time without you realizing it. There is a lot of unraveling that needs to take place for us to fully heal.

I was also experiencing many symptoms of Complex Post-Traumatic Stress Disorder (CPTSD), which is common after being in a relationship with someone with narcissistic personality disorder.

Most of us have heard of PTSD, but the recognition of Complex Post-Traumatic Stress Disorder is fairly recent in the world of psychology.

PTSD is an anxiety disorder that can develop after a person experiences a traumatic event. Complex PTSD is a result of prolonged or repeated trauma over a period of months or years.

Here are some common symptoms of Complex PTSD:
- reliving trauma through flashbacks and nightmares
- dizziness or nausea when recalling memories

- avoiding situations or places that remind you of the trauma or abuser
- hyperarousal, which means being in a continual state of high alert
- the belief that the world is a dangerous place, a loss of faith and belief in the goodness of others
- a loss of trust in yourself or others
- difficulty sleeping
- being jumpy—sensitive to stimuli
- hypervigilance—constantly observing others' behavior, searching for signs of bad behavior and clues that reveal bad intentions
- low self-esteem, a lack of self-confidence
- emotional regulation difficulties—you find yourself being more emotionally triggered than your usual way of being; you may experience intense anger or sadness or have thoughts of suicide
- preoccupation with an abuser—it is not uncommon to fixate on the abuser, the relationship with the abuser, or getting revenge for the abuse
- detachment from others—wanting to isolate yourself, withdraw from life
- challenges in relationships, including difficulty trusting others, possibly seeking out a rescuer, or even getting into another relationship with an abuser because it is familiar
- disassociation—feeling detached from yourself and your emotions
- depression—sadness and low energy, a lack of motivation
- toxic guilt and shame—a feeling that somehow you deserved to be abused, or that your failure to leave earlier is a sign of weakness

- destructive self-harming behavior—abusing drugs and alcohol is a common result of ongoing trauma; this can also include overeating to soothe and self-medicate. The flip side can be harming yourself through not eating. These behaviors develop during the period of trauma as a way to deal with or forget about the trauma and emotional pain.

Symptoms of Complex PTSD can vary, and they may change over time.

Reading this list and seeing many symptoms you may be experiencing can feel daunting and discouraging. Instead of viewing this from a perspective of despair, I encourage you to see it as validation, and let yourself breathe a sigh of relief, knowing now that there is a reason for everything you are feeling and experiencing.

The good news is there is a way out. I am not a fan of the word "disorder" because it can make us feel like we are stuck with this, like this is who we are now. The truth is your body is amazing and capable of complete healing and restoration.

If you think you have CPTSD, I recommend finding practitioners who know how to help people heal from the effects of this type of trauma. When you interview therapists or coaches who work with CPTSD, make sure you feel emotionally safe with them. Say yes to the ones who you notice your body feeling relaxed and free to be yourself with, and walk away if your body feels tense, unsafe, or muddled around them. Remember, you are in charge of your healing. Be choosy with who you hire to help you heal.

When you experience ongoing trauma, your nervous system is affected. I will talk more extensively about trauma and the nervous system later in this book. You will learn several exercises to help regulate your autonomic nervous system that are an essential part of healing after these relationships. These exercises will also help with CPTSD.

You have been through a lot. Recognize this and be incredibly tender with yourself as you take steps to heal.

In my new place, I continued to seek out support, advice, and more information. I also continued to receive abusive emails. As you probably know by now, abuse from a narcissist does not end when the relationship ends. I also received a devastating email from one of his flying monkeys during this time. This is a term used to describe people who act in abusive ways on behalf of the narcissist. The trauma that coursed through my body as I read these messages is difficult to describe, but I imagine if you have been with a narcissist, you will know the debilitating feeling that comes from reading emails, texts, and messages from them. It is a physical sensation that instantly takes over your body and leaves you emotionally paralyzed.

These emails also left me with a tremendous amount of self-doubt, wondering if their words were true. Even though my eyes were continuing to open to the truth, I would still wonder if I really did have so many things wrong with me, if I had been a difficult person to live with and was blind to this about myself.

The barrage of toxic cruelty over time depletes you of your life-force energy and for many of us, makes us question if we want to keep going. If we even want to be here anymore.

It was during this time that I reached that place. My soul, heart, and body were depleted. I no longer felt I had a reason to be here. Nothing about life felt like I wanted to be a part of it anymore. It felt like there was nothing left for me here. In my depression I could not see beyond the thick and hazy clouds that had enveloped me. My belief in my worthiness to enjoy any happiness in life was gone. I even had moments of deluding myself into believing everyone would be okay without me. Sure, some would cry at first, but in time, they would all be fine, I thought. This, of course, could not have been further from the truth, but when you get to those deep places of despair like I did, you can't think or see clearly.

There are so many stories to tell that would help you understand all that contributed to bringing me to these depths of despair, but for my own safety I do not feel free to share the details of what I experienced. However, I do want to share with you how I felt during this time in my life, in hopes that if you are feeling the same way right now, you will know you are not alone. And you will know this feeling and state of being is temporary, and there is a big, beautiful light at the end of this tunnel of pain and despair. Keep going. Keep choosing to be here. Life will get better. You won't always feel this way.

You deserve to be here. We want you here. You have a right to be here on this planet. You have a place here that only you can fill. Anyone who treats you in a way that causes you to question that is wrong and does not deserve your time, energy, and attention.

If you have considered taking your own life, please reach out to a therapist or mental health care worker right away. At the very least, a trusted friend. Tell somebody. You don't have to walk this road alone. You are worthy and deserving of feeling good and having a life that is beautiful and brings you joy. Healing is possible. You will get through this. You will feel different one day. There is life beyond the clouds you feel right now. This will pass and you are going to be just fine. You are incredibly strong. You will see this more and more as time goes on.

With the clarity I have now, I can say with absolute confidence that all the cruel and negative messages I received from others about me were 100 percent false. The truth is I am a beautiful soul. I am kind. I am loving. I am honest. I am sensitive. I am considerate. I am a great listener. I am compassionate. I am giving. I am strong. I am worthy of respect, kindness, and love, and so are you. Please let these words wash over you because they are what is true. You are a glorious human being, and my wish for you is to be able to see that.

You deserve to be treated in a way that brings you life, in a way where what flows through your body feels like pure joy, love, and compassion. This is what you were made for, and this is what you deserve.

Over time, as I took care of myself and sought help from professionals, my depression passed. Yours will too. Do the things you need right now that feel supportive and nurturing to you. Be with people who love and support you, and leave the rest. You deserve to feel good. You deserve to be treated well. Take exquisite care of your precious heart. You are wanted and needed here.

CHAPTER THREE

Running Away and Learning How to Take Care of My Heart

O VER TIME, MY DEPRESSION BECAME LESS INTENSE, but I still experienced a sense of feeling lost. I asked myself one day what I craved. I love that question for times we feel lost. I learned it during the life-coach training I had taken years before. When I tuned in to what I craved, the only thing I could get in touch with was a desire to run away from my life.

I wanted to run far, far away to a place that looked nothing like home. Somewhere no one knew me. Somewhere I had never been before. Bali kept coming to mind. I mentioned this to my dad in passing once, not thinking it was possible, just dreaming. I wasn't sure how I could swing it financially and with the responsibilities I had. But the thought of staring at rice fields with no one around and crying for as long as I needed sounded so nurturing and therapeutic. Not being responsible for anyone but myself sounded glorious. Decadent.

A couple months passed, and one day I received an email from my dad. He told me he had a friend who owned a villa in Bali, and they said I could stay there for free! "What? Are you serious?" *Was it okay for me to do something so deliciously lavish*? This felt so extrav-agant, so indulgent. Out of curiosity, I looked up flights. The prices were lower than I'd seen before when I was daydreaming. I called my sister, "What do you think? Should I go?"

"Yes, go!" she said with an exuberant smile I could feel all over my body.

A couple months later I was standing in a villa in Ubud, Bali overlooking a rice field.

Travel has always been one of my most favorite types of therapy. As soon as the plane takes off, I feel anxiety wash away and a joyous smile takes over. Life springs up inside me and I feel as if anything is possible. I am reminded of how big and wonderful the world is.

It felt amazing to just be with myself. To wake up every morning and ask what sounded good to me in that moment.

I had read *Eat, Pray, Love* years ago and loved every second of it. Knowing I was going to be in the same city in Bali where Elizabeth Gilbert, the author of that book, stayed I determined I wanted to meet Ketut, the Balinese medicine man she talked so much about in her book.

When I went to see him, another man greeted me and told me Ketut was too old to do readings now, and he would be the one talking to me and telling me what he "saw" for me. I was able to sit next to sweet Ketut and hold his hands and see and feel his smile, which lit up my soul. He felt kind. The other man did as well. It felt healing and calming to sit with two gentle men who cared about my heart. Even if they said nothing, just their loving presence and authenticity was healing.

The man closed his eyes, took a breath, then looked at the palm of my hand. His face turned to concern as he said, "Last relationship not good. Very confusing. Not good for your heart." He knew nothing about me when he said that. I could feel tears welling up in me. After being treated so badly for so long, there is something about having someone "see" you, and feeling their care, compassion, and kindness that is incredibly healing. After telling me more of what he saw, he ended by repeating over and over, "You must take care of your heart. When your heart happy, more happy come to you. You must take care of your heart."

With all the therapy techniques out there, I think the most powerful for all of us is to be seen, heard, and cared for. When we feel that, we feel safe. There is nothing more healing than that, in my mind. Love and safety. A powerful and restorative combination.

The medicine men's kindness opened a floodgate in me that was ready to be felt. When I got back to the villa I collapsed on the floor in the corner of my room and sobbed, deep, guttural sobbing. It was the kind of crying where you know you are releasing pain that has been there for a very long time. I could tell the depth of these tears came from places in me that included this relationship, as well as things I'd experienced in years prior. These tears were a buildup of an entire lifetime of narcissistic abuse. Curled up in the fetal position, I let the dam burst inside me and cried for as long as I needed.

The words *You must take care of your heart* kept playing in my mind. My tears felt like they represented deep grief for the girl in me, the woman in me whose heart had not been taken care of, valued, or respected. When you live with narcissists you get the message that your heart does not matter. You learn to not trust it. You learn to bury it deep within you. It is seen as a nuisance, a burden. It is viewed as being too much, wanting too much, feeling too much. You are seen as too dramatic. Too sensitive. Too needy.

I found myself saying, "I'm sorry. I'm so sorry," over and over to the girl in me who had been wounded so deeply, to the woman in me who had been through so much. I began to apologize for my part in this too, for all the times I hadn't listened to my heart. For all the times I had not trusted it. I knew this wasn't my fault. I didn't blame myself. The fact that I had neglected my heart for so many years was understandable. I was groomed and trained to do that. It was a natural result of experiencing different narcissists who had played significant roles throughout my life. I felt compassion and a determination to change the way I treated myself, to become a fierce protector of my heart.

I spoke to my heart that day, as if it was a young girl—a beautiful, frightened, wounded girl who needed to feel safe, loved, and cherished. I told her things would be different from here on out. I would listen to her. I would not put her down for anything anymore. I would honor her feelings and her desires. I would respect her intuition, her gut feelings. I would not talk her out of how she feels. I would accept her and love her with an unconditional and bold love. It was time to heal this heart I held in my hands. I wanted her to live in a body where she felt safe, seen, and held. I wanted to become a trusted refuge for myself. I wanted to be the first place I would turn when I needed someone to listen to me and love me.

When I returned home, I set about making it my top priority to change the way I treated myself. With this new resolve, the following year became my Cocooning phase, which resulted in profound healing for me and helped to build the foundation for the way I am with myself now. My heart became my priority and I continue to check in with it daily, moment to moment. It is the gentle and compassionate leader of my life now. It is fierce, it is wise, it is tender, and it is strong, and over time I have fallen madly in love with it.

I began to live my days checking in with my heart often, asking it how it was doing. What was it feeling? What did it need? If I was tired, I honored my body and would lie down. If I felt lost, I would sit with that feeling, allowing and accepting everything I felt. I chose not to judge myself, not to see myself as there being anything wrong with me. If I felt sadness, grief, anger, I would stop what I was doing and ask myself what I needed.

Sometimes I would wrap myself in a blanket, curl up on the sofa, and let myself cry. Sometimes I would play music if that felt nurturing, soothing, and caretaking. I didn't leave my house very often. I felt held there. The world did not feel safe enough for me to venture out past my four walls yet. The grocery store, taking my kids to and from school, and the nearby mountains were the main places

I ventured to for a time. They were my places of solace. I felt cradled when I sat under trees. It helped me think through things to walk trails where I didn't see many people. I wasn't ready for people yet. I needed to cocoon and be with myself.

Life still happened. There were things to do, responsibilities I had, but I kept my life as simple as I possibly could.

I found myself being led to different things that helped me heal. One day an idea came to me to gather all my photo albums and take time to look at pictures of myself at different ages. I would look into my eyes and talk to myself as if that age of me was sitting right in front of me. I would acknowledge what I was going through at that time in my life, and I would tell that age Debbie that she was beautiful, that she was worthy of love, kindness, and respect.

I looked at photos of myself at different points during my previous relationship and did the same thing. I saw how the light behind my eyes had dimmed. I saw myself feeling lost, confused, and unlovable. I would say things like, "Oh Debbie, I'm so sorry. You can't see right now what you are going through. You deserve so much better. You will get through this, and you will feel better one day, brighter, more like your true self. I love you. I cherish you. I'm so proud of you. You are amazing." I could feel my body relax a little more each time I talked to my past self in this way. This exercise contributed to helping me rewrite the destructive and untrue messages I had received.

I also began doing "mirror work" as a way of connecting to myself. I originally heard of the concept of looking in a mirror and saying affirmations from Louise Hay. I took that idea and instead of affirmations, I used it to engage with myself, to check in with my heart. It may sound simple, and it is, but it's also incredibly powerful. When no one else is around, you look into your eyes and give yourself full permission to be exactly where you are, to feel whatever you are feeling. You can notice very quickly what emotions you are feeling. For some people, this can be an overwhelming experience, especially if you are not used to being with your emotions. If you find this to be true for yourself, do this in small doses. You don't want to overwhelm yourself if this is new and uncomfortable. Be gentle with yourself with everything you do. You've been through a lot and gentleness, compassion, and kindness is what you need now to heal.

For some this might look like just taking a peek into your eyes. You will most likely feel emotions come up right away. Then maybe put the mirror down and just let yourself feel, telling yourself whatever you are feeling is okay and you are safe. Here is an example of what it looked like for me. I would look into my eyes. I would see sadness. I would see fear in my eyes. I would see anger. I would see grief. I would often cry. I would make sure I looked into my eyes with compassion and empathy and would say things such as, "I see your sadness. It's understandable. Go ahead and feel it. It's okay. You can let it out. You are safe now. I won't leave you. I am here and I love you." Then I would let myself cry.

If I saw anger in my eyes, I might say something like, "I see that anger in you. And it's okay. You have every right and reason to be angry. Anger is okay. It's normal. It's natural. I love you. It's okay to let it out...let me know what you need. I'm here for you. I love you." Then I might go punch the punching bag we had in our basement, or I might go into nature, or scream, or pound my fists on my bed and yell, or turn on loud music and stomp and dance. I would listen to what felt good to my body and do that.

I should mention I would only do mirror work when my kids were at school or out with friends. I needed the freedom to fully let go, and I didn't want them to take on anything I was feeling. This was my healing to take care of for myself. My responsibility. Not theirs or anyone else's.

That year, I did many more activities based on my own inner guidance. It was like my heart was leading me on this path of healing and I was developing a very tender and special relationship with myself. I was relearning what it meant, what it looked like to be loved unconditionally.

One day I was sharing the things I was doing and discovering with a friend of mine and she said, "You should write these things down. It would really help people. You live your life very differently and it would be great to share all you are learning and experiencing with others." I loved the idea that my experience might be able to help others with their pain too. So, that's what I did. I began writing down all the exercises I did over that year. They added up to 21 healing exercises. I recorded them along with personal stories I experienced and together, they became my first book, *The Safest Place Possible: A Guide to Healing and Transformation*.

Truthfully, I didn't expect many people to read it, since I was virtually unknown to the world at that time, but it was helpful for me to write it all down. Even if I helped a few, that felt worth it to me. Little did I know that a few years later I would hear from a woman who called it her favorite book of all time. You never know where your life will take you when you follow your heart and do the things that not only heal you, but help heal others as well.

Another exercise I started doing that felt so nurturing to me after experiencing so much judgment from others and myself I aptly named, "No judgment, Debbie." I listed insecurities and fears I had and then followed them by saying, "No judgment, Debbie." As with all the exercises, my body would always feel more and more relaxed as I said the words. It looked something like this: I would first be honest about what I was thinking, which was often some form of harsh attack on myself. When you experience narcissistic abuse, you learn to be hard on yourself. You learn to punish yourself instead of giving yourself grace.

Here are some examples of things I would say at the time:

"I should be saving more money."

    "No judgment, Debbie."

"I should be using my time more wisely."

    "No judgment, Debbie."

"I should be eating better."

    "No judgment, Debbie."

"Maybe he's right. Maybe I am lazy. Maybe I do self-sabotage. Maybe I was really hard to live with."

    "No judgment, Debbie."

"Why can't I get it together? Why does life feel so hard for me? So many other people seem to do just fine. What's wrong with me?"

    "No judgment, Debbie."

"I should be further along in life by now."

    "No judgment, Debbie."

"I hate that I'm still overweight. Why can't I be more disciplined?"

    "No judgment, Debbie."

"I should be more healed by now."

    "No judgment, Debbie."

I would do this often, when I found myself saying things that were not loving to myself. Each time I said the words, "No judgment, Debbie," I said them in a gentle and reassuring tone, so my body, my heart, would not only hear them, but fully feel the unconditional love with which I intended to fill myself. It was my way of saying, "It's okay. You are okay. All your feelings are okay. You are perfect just the way you are. There is nothing to feel bad about. You are valuable and wanted exactly the way you are right now. There is nothing you need to change for you to be worthy of love and kindness."

After a year of consistently bathing myself in loving exercises I realized the cruel voice that had been present inside me for so many years, who had spoken to me so harshly and judgmentally, was gone.

It was gone completely, never to return. I noticed I no longer spoke to myself in demeaning and berating ways. That was not allowed anymore. I had built a foundation of love for myself, of safety. I had built trust. This new foundation would keep strengthening in me over time and carry me through some difficult things that were to come.

CHAPTER FOUR

A Deeper Layer of Healing

A FTER SPENDING THAT YEAR NURTURING MYSELF, I reached a deeper level of healing where I was ready to look at the part I had played in the relationship I'd been in. The covert abuse I experienced was difficult to recognize, but when I looked back, especially when I read through my journals, there were many ways I was treated, even in the beginning, that were unkind and disrespectful. Yet somehow, I excused the behavior. I was beginning to realize that I had tolerated covert emotional abuse for most of my life from several people, and the question I wanted to answer for myself was, "Why was I okay with being treated that way?" I knew I needed to understand this to fully heal and to have a chance at future healthy, loving relationships. I did not want to keep repeating this pattern.

I started exploring what in my life led to me not being able to see through this behavior. I had no judgment for myself. I just wanted to understand, so I could heal and correct the beliefs in me that led me to be okay with subtle abuse.

I was able to see where I had experienced narcissistic traits in my childhood and how this set me up to end up with covert narcissists. When we experience abusive behavior growing up, we get used to that way of treatment and see it as normal, and often end up with someone who is similar to the person or people we experienced. Sometimes they may appear to be different, but in fact are another version of the same. For instance, if you grew up with an overt narcissist and end up dating a covert narcissist, you feel relieved at first that you found someone who behaves differently from your mom or dad. Years later you realize you were experiencing the same thing you did in your childhood, but this time the abuse was more subtle, so you didn't see it. You also experience an unconscious feeling of familiarity, which brings you comfort. You know this dance. You know how to be the one who puts others first, and deep down doesn't believe you deserve pure, unconditional love. You are familiar with having someone project their issues onto you and have been conditioned to willingly take responsibility for them.

During this time, when I was recovering from my most recent relationship, I feared dating again. I didn't trust myself to be able to see through covert behavior. I realized I needed to reteach myself love so I would be able to recognize the counterfeit. I needed to keep being a loving presence for myself so that I would get so used to what real love looks and feels like that my body would be able to discern behavior that felt different from the love I was now used to. This is why it is so important for us to practice treating ourselves with kindness, compassion, absolute acceptance, and self-love.

To help you gain your own clarity with this, below are some questions to begin exploring for yourself. Feel free to write down any thoughts or insights that come to you as to what may have contributed to you getting involved with a narcissist. Keep in mind this is not about blaming. There is nothing in yourself to blame. This is about understanding to gain wisdom and insight for future relationships.

1. Looking back, what patterns are similar to what you have experienced in your relationship with a narcissist? Did either of your parents project their issues onto you? Was there gaslighting? Did you feel like you were never enough? Or maybe too much? Too sensitive? Was the focus on their emotions and their needs and yours were not important? Use this space to brainstorm anything that may come to mind.

2. What unhealthy or destructive messages about yourself did you receive growing up? What similar messages did you receive from the narcissist in your life?

3. How did you feel around your mom growing up? How did you feel around your dad? Are any of those feelings or bodily sensations the same as those prompted by a current narcissist in your life?

4. How did your mom treat your dad? How did your dad treat your mom? If you had same-sex parents, how did they treat each other? Do you see any similarities with how you are treated by the narcissist in your life?

_____

_____

_____

_____

_____

_____

_____

_____

_____

_____

_____

_____

_____

_____

_____

_____

_____

_____

_____

_____

_____

_____

_____

_____

_____

5. The space below is for any other thoughts that may come to mind that help give you clarity as you begin to unravel things in your childhood that may have set you up for relationships with narcissists. Keep in mind, even very subtle messages, even well-intentioned but unhealthy behaviors, will reinforce future unhealthy behavior we learn to accept as normal as adults.

CHAPTER FIVE

Relentless Attacks and the Rise of a Life-Changing Decision

OUT OF THE DARKNESS CAME THE LIGHT.

As I imagine you probably know by now, even after the relationship is over, narcissists rarely leave you alone. You can be the target of their rage for years after, even when you try and cut off or minimize contact. If you have children with them and need to have contact, they will use this connection to continue to try and abuse you emotionally and psychologically.

It can feel as if you are making empowering strides in your healing and then one email, text, or interaction with them can seem like it sets you back months or years. This happened to me, many times. One particular email, years after the breakup, affected me in ways I hadn't experienced with previous ones. Yet it also became the catalyst for strength to rise in me like never before.

I received this abusive email more than three years after the relationship ended.

This time I recognized the abuse and stood up for myself. I placed a boundary. I wrote back and said if I received any more abusive emails, I would need to block him.

About an hour after my brief, unemotional, just-the-facts, direct response I received a three-page reply. It was a fire hose of attacks, and as I read it I felt the waves of trauma flood through me.

There was something about the words in that email, combined with the intensity and overwhelm of the previous years, that did something to my body I hadn't experienced before. I sank into a quiet internal state and didn't speak for three days. I felt like my body was shutting down and all my systems felt like they were simultaneously turning out the lights. I sat in a chair in the corner of my living room and stared out the window each day for long periods of time. I felt like I couldn't move, like all life had been drained from my body, and I was now just a shell, just existing. I felt numb.

I would go to bed at night and wake up feeling the same way, then, as I lay there, emotions would come rushing out of me. I would roll over and sob for a long time. I woke up every morning like this for three days. The third morning something different happened. I began by rolling over on my side and crying. After all the tears came out, as I lay in bed a different feeling began to emerge. I thought of all the cruelty I had endured. I knew I wasn't alone. I thought of all the other people who were experiencing the same thing. I felt how wrong this all was. A fierceness began to rise in me, a strength from deep within. I closed my eyes and an image appeared in my mind's eye. It was a cover of a book with big bold capital letters that read, "THE COVERT PASSIVE AGGRESSIVE NARCISSIST." It felt like an invitation. Like someone was saying, "Will you? Will you write the book?"

I knew if I accepted this invitation, I would give it my all and make it the best book I possibly could. In that moment, everything felt quiet. I felt connected to others like me who were going through this. I felt a responsibility to them, a calling to make this the most helpful book I possibly could, so they could get the clarity they deserved. I knew this book needed to be written. Nothing like it existed. It was time and I was ready. With my eyes closed, lying in my bed that morning, with the feeling of a warrior about to go to battle expanding inside me, I said, "Okay. I will write it. And I will make it great."

I was done being sad, I decided. I was done feeling powerless. I was done taking this abuse. I cleared plans I had made that year and dedicated my time to this important project, and nothing else.

I began planning. I didn't want the book to be just me telling my story. I wanted it to address all types of relationships and include other people's experiences too. I also wanted to make sure it was accurate. I decided I would interview lots of people who had experienced covert narcissistic abuse and would find and interview therapists who specialize in this area. I would read even more material on the subject. I would dig up all the journals I'd kept since the beginning of the relationship and review them for things I hadn't seen at the time.

I asked people in a local support group for those who had experienced narcissistic abuse if they would be willing to meet with me and share their stories. So many bravely opened up to me and told me details of the horrific relationships they had been in. I often felt like I was looking in a mirror as they shared so many of the same things I had. It was validating and helpful for my own journey of sorting out what I had been through and was still going through.

I also asked the life-coaching group I was a part of if any of them had been through this and would be willing to be interviewed. One person would lead me to another. I ended up hearing from people all over the world. The cultures were different, but the essence of the experiences was the same.

My eyes opened even more to things I hadn't seen previously. During the writing of the book, I ended a friendship after realizing that person was also a covert narcissist. My ability to recognize covert narcissistic traits heightened. I was so grateful to all the people who were willing to share their vulnerable and painful stories. When we come together and share, a tremendous amount of healing happens for all of us and a special connection is formed. Only those who have gone through this can really understand, and there is an immediate bond that is felt, a feeling of safety.

Reading through my old journals as research was one of the most eye-opening experiences for me. I was now able to see all the times I had excused hurtful and disrespectful behavior throughout the relationship. My jaw dropped as I read entries I had written from the very beginning, even during the love bombing stage. Treatment of me that was so horrific, and things I would never accept now. I felt tremendous compassion for myself, for enduring so much that I didn't realize at the time. My love for myself and fierce protectiveness for my own well-being grew more and more as my understanding of the abuse I had experienced became even clearer.

CHAPTER SIX

Learning the Balance of Giving and Receiving

EVEN THOUGH I KNEW I WAS ON THE RIGHT PATH, I experienced tremendous anxiety and fear as I was writing the book. I would picture people in my life who had NPD reading it. I could hear the judgments they would say against me. I tried to find ways to help give me courage and safety as I wrote. At one point I decided to put a picture of my best friend, Liz, next to my laptop so I could look at her when I felt fear and see her loving face looking back at me as I typed. I would imagine I was simply explaining to her what a covert narcissist is. This helped my body feel safe.

I would also write putting my focus on the reader, which often brought me to tears. I knew they would be in pain trying to figure out what was happening in their life, experiencing cognitive dissonance, and doubting themselves as I had for so long. They were in my awareness the whole time I wrote the book, and they gave me strength to keep going. I wanted to help them as much as I possibly could. I knew they deserved that just like I did.

When the book came out my body started to not feel well from a buildup of all the stress of writing it and fearing what may happen after it came out. I had fears of the possible repercussions I might experience for going public with the book. I wondered if I might be "punished" as narcissists do when they experience a narcissistic injury. This is a term used to explain what happens when you place boundaries on the narcissist, stand up to them, or confront or expose them. Their narcissistic rage is triggered and they unleash it at the person they perceive is threatening their reputation.

After a few weeks of my body feeling worse and worse and having symptoms I hadn't had before, I went to the doctor to find out what was going on. I discovered I had dangerously high blood pressure. He immediately put me on medication. He was alarmed when he saw the numbers and told me I had "stroke-level" blood pressure. He instructed me to go home and do nothing but rest until the numbers went down.

I am one who does not take well to medication. I once took a half of a common over-the-counter cold and flu relief pill and felt like a truck had run over me. My body is highly sensitive in many areas of life. I get overwhelmed by crowds of people and my body feels anxious and agitated around loud noises. I can't walk down the aisle of the grocery store that is filled with laundry detergent, because the smell of the chemicals is too much for me. I am sensitive emotionally, and also in ways where I sometimes know or sense things before they happen. I have an acute intuition. I was grateful to the medication for keeping me from dying or having a stroke, but I also knew I wanted to learn how to lower my blood pressure naturally. Over the next several months I researched how to do that. I changed the way I ate and took a few short walks every day. I worked on my thoughts more, making a conscious effort to focus on positive things more than my fears.

As I began to get my energy back, I started a YouTube channel to get the word out about my book and to give people more helpful and clear information about covert narcissism. I began receiving requests to be interviewed on other people's channels and podcasts. I later hired someone to translate the book into Spanish.

After time and changing things in my life to heal my body, I was able to wean off the blood pressure medication. As I was feeling more energy, my attention was drawn to books and other projects I was dreaming up. I envisioned creating healing retreats where survivors could all gather in a peaceful, natural place and do healing things together.

I decided to create online courses to help get more information out there. Over time I started doing coaching sessions with people and felt honored to meet others who were so willing to open their heart to me. I loved loving them and helping validate their experience.

Some people reached out to me and said they wanted to read the book, but didn't want the narcissist in their life to see it. So I decided to record audio versions of both of my books so people would have that option.

I continued to film more videos for YouTube, and later began an online support group.

My life, after years of cocooning on and off, had rapidly become very busy and very full. With all of that came new lessons around boundaries and self-care. I would need to learn a healthy balance of giving and receiving.

One thing I have found with people who end up with narcissists is that most of us have an innate desire to give, to help. This is a beautiful quality we naturally inhabit. Most of us were not raised in healthy environments where we were taught or shown how to navigate life as natural nurtures, healers, and lovers. Some of us were raised in households with narcissists who exploited this trait. Some of us were raised by well-meaning parents who gave too much of themselves, and didn't have their own healthy boundaries, or we had a parent who drained others by becoming a "martyr," giving to others as a way of seeking attention. Many of us received the message that we were here to serve, that this is what made us valuable, this was our role, and anything that became about us was selfish. We were taught by words or example that draining yourself by giving to others was a highly regarded behavior to which we should aspire.

These dynamics likely contributed to us getting into relationships with people who abuse the beautiful, natural traits we have, and we don't recognize it because we weren't taught what healthy looks like when it comes to giving, receiving, and boundaries. We weren't shown examples of a healthy balance. We didn't get the message that our mental health was important and that our purpose here is not to drain ourselves for others. This was about to become a big lesson for me as I relearned what healthy giving looks like.

As my book on narcissism was introduced to more readers, I began receiving private messages on social media platforms. My email inboxes were filled with heart-wrenching letters from people all over the world telling me their stories and asking me for help. I would read daily posts from people in the online support group I had recently started and began to notice how my body felt as I read each one. Since their stories were so similar to mine, I could feel myself being retraumatized as I read one after another. I had to close my laptop and lie down. I could feel the life in me being drained, and I thought, Oh no. What have I done? Should I have started this group? Am I really ready to facilitate something that is so close to my own pain? Maybe I'm not healed enough…

I wanted to close my blinds, curl up with a blanket, and shut out the world again.

I knew I didn't want to close the group. It would feel like I was abandoning them. I was hearing from so many who were so grateful for the support and getting so much help from it. I would feel awful ending it. I wanted to figure out a way to keep it going, to do what I could to monitor it, and keep it a safe place to share and connect, while still making sure my own health didn't decline. I realized I couldn't do this alone and needed help. I needed people I could trust. I put out my desire and intention to the universe and life sent me Linda Barnes, a beautiful, kind soul from the UK who had emailed me with a question about narcissism. This started a conversation between us that grew to many more and eventually turned into a cherished friendship. She joined the group as my lead admin, which helped take the full responsibility of the group off my shoulders and enabled me to keep it going. She had experienced narcissistic abuse as well, and had done a lot of her own research and healing. Her wisdom and heart have helped make the group a very special gathering, and her support and friendship have been an unexpected gift and blessing in my life. With her help I was able to keep the group going and still take care of my own heart.

Through all the difficulties, life seemed to keep sending me the right people at just the right time.

I was also beginning to learn that it was okay for me to not respond to everyone. It was okay for me to disappoint people. In fact, it was essential. I am one person, and I can only do so much. I had to look out for myself while I was helping others. A big lesson I learned and am still learning is the more I take care of myself, the better I can help others. I learned to put up boundaries as to how available I could be for others. I learned to look at different projects I was involved in and ask myself which ones were draining me, and which ones brought me more life. I learned to only say yes to people who requested interviews with me if they felt good to me. My body knew and I always ended up regretting the invitations I didn't feel good about but thought I "should" accept. Likewise, I always ended up enjoying the interviews where my body immediately lit up the moment the person asked me.

I was learning that I deserved to have a life that felt good.

It took me years to get comfortable saying the words, "I deserve." After decades of narcissistic abuse from significant people in my life, I couldn't even say the words, "I deserve to be happy," or, "I deserve love and respect," or, "I deserve to live a life I love." This is the effect of this type of abuse. You get to a place where you don't even feel deserving of basic needs in life.

I began reassessing everything in my life. People I spent time with, activities I was involved in, and where I was living. I questioned whether I wanted to stay in Colorado. Did I feel alive here? The more I sat with this question, the more I realized the answer was no.

There is a mix of painful and good memories for me in Colorado. I loved the mountains, but had always dreamed of living by the ocean too. I longed for water, flowers, fall leaves, and a lower elevation.

I needed a gentle, quiet place. I craved an area that had fewer people and more nature. I now knew I wanted to build a life helping others through writing books and creating other things that would help others heal. To do this, I knew I needed to live in a place that felt restful, that felt like a retreat. I needed a place where my heart felt held and supported so I could do all the things I wanted to do in the world. Colorado Springs, where I had been living, as well as being a place filled with memories, was getting more and more populated and I found it difficult to get quiet there and listen.

My son decided he wanted to leave Colorado with me, so after months of both of us exploring ideas of where we may want to live, we ended up being drawn to a little town in Oregon called Ashland.

We took a trip out there to see how it felt and how we felt when we were there. It turned out to be everything we were both looking for. It was a gentle, small town filled with so many different types of trees and flowers. There was a lake nearby and a stream that ran through a downtown park that went on for miles. At the top of the park were pools of water that are known as the fairy ponds. The city was filled with artists, writers, singers, and people who wanted calm. I would later discover it is a place that draws people who want to heal. And it was about a 90-minute drive from the ocean.

On our visit, we walked through Lithia Park in downtown Ashland and passed a man playing his cello. People were sitting on benches. Some were lying on blankets spread throughout a soft grassy area filled with trees and the sound of the nearby stream. Later we saw a man playing a harp. I stood there and began to cry as I looked around. No one was in a hurry. They were all there soaking up the peaceful sounds. My son, seeing the tears well up in me, said, "Well, I think we have our answer."

We flew back home. I sold and gave away most of my belongings, and we filled a small trailer and headed west.

My time in Ashland would be much different than I expected, and much more difficult than I had ever dreamed. Yet it would bring about the transformation and deep healing I had been wanting.

CHAPTER SEVEN

Learning to Trust My Own Guidance as My Health Fell Apart

A FTER ABOUT A MONTH OF BEING IN ASHLAND, my health fell apart. When we seek healing, deep, profound, long-lasting healing, sometimes it comes in ways we don't expect, ways that are much more challenging than we anticipate. My plan was to feel peace, rest, write this very book you have in your hands, and continue my healing path in a calm and peaceful way. Life had a different plan for me that would ultimately teach me things I needed to realize for me to fully heal all parts of me. My journey in Ashland would be shorter than expected and more turbulent, but I am so grateful for it now. I also believe I was kept from completing this book at that time because I needed to learn more essential information that I now see is highly important for healing after narcissistic abuse, both for myself and so that I could share with you.

I understand now that my health fell apart for several reasons. After so many years of trauma to my body, mind, and spirit, I was finally in a place where I could let down. I didn't know anyone there, so I had a break from being with people, and a chance to just be with myself. Ashland became a second significant cocooning time for me. The quiet allowed me to exhale, and my body could feel it was safe and free to fully let out all that had been building up in me after so many years of abuse.

The lessons I was about to learn had to do with trusting myself and not giving my power away to anyone, even "the experts." I would also be led to research the effects of abuse on the nervous system and how to regulate the autonomic nervous system. I was going to learn deeper ways of taking care of myself, as well as letting go and trusting life when things appear to be falling apart.

One area in my life where I have had tremendous fear for years, and have given my power away to others, is with my health.

Soon after moving to Ashland, my cousin in Colorado had a stroke. He was airlifted to a hospital. He lost the ability to speak normally, to walk, and to be able to do so many things that come naturally to us. When I talked with him on the phone a few days later, he spoke slowly. He told me I need to make sure I was taking blood pressure medication. I got off the phone and checked my blood pressure with the machine I had bought years ago when I first had what the doctor told me were stroke-level numbers. It was higher than it had ever been. I immediately went to see a doctor and she gave me a prescription. All the pharmacies were closed, so I had to wait until the next day to pick up the pills.

That night I was filled with fear. I talked on the phone to my dad, who was very concerned about me, which raised my anxiety even more. I tried to calm myself, talk to myself, listen to calming music, pray, and recite affirmations. I determined to eat only foods that would help me heal. I searched "emotional reasons behind high blood pressure" on the internet so I could learn what the underlying cause was and address it. I came across an article by Dr. Christiane Northrup that talked about high blood pressure being linked to trauma stuck in the body. I determined I would find a way to release all trauma from my body.

The next morning my son went to pick up the medication for me. When he handed me the familiar bag, I looked at it, held it, and something rose in my body. "No," I told myself. "I can't do it. I can't take this. I will heal myself."

Before I continue my story, I need to add a disclaimer. I am not a healthcare professional. I am not here to give you advice for your body. You are in charge of your own body and each of our paths are different. My intention in sharing this is to talk about an important healing aspect for myself after experiencing narcissistic abuse, not to give out health or medical advice. You need to take whatever path is the best for you. What you need in your health journey may be different from what I chose to do.

For me in that moment, I determined to find another way to heal. I knew I had lowered my blood pressure on my own before and I was sure I could do it again.

Another reason I had moved to Ashland is because it is a place that attracts healers and people who are into natural ways of supporting the body. I spent the day looking up different types of healing modalities and practitioners in the area. I began calling people and scheduling appointments. I met with a chiropractor who specialized in Chinese medicine. I tried wave therapy, where a sound machine emits low-frequency acoustic pressure waves to help reduce inflammation, which has been known to help lower blood pressure. I met with an acupuncturist who practiced Five Element acupuncture, which I had experienced before in Colorado and it had produced good results. I even found a massage therapist who literally works with people who have experienced narcissistic abuse and does a technique that helps release trauma from the body! When she first saw me, she told me I looked familiar and then realized she had seen a few of my videos on YouTube about covert narcissism! I was amazed!

I did a lot of my own research on trauma and the ways to release it from the body. One thing I read was that releasing emotions can help lower blood pressure. So, I let myself cry, a lot. My sole purpose each day became about healing myself. The stakes were high. My life was on the line and at that point nothing else mattered. I tried to talk myself through my fears, which were now heightened even more. The way I was feeling, I couldn't coach, so I closed my practice.

I didn't have the energy to write or do anything that would generate income that would support my son and me. I was forced to trust life to take care of me. I had to let go of fear, because that fear was affecting my body.

I became vigilant about my thoughts and beliefs, trying to keep them as positive and empowering as I possibly could. I knew how powerful and helpful this was to the body. I could feel it and had done research for years on the power of our thoughts. I noticed after talking to family members my blood pressure would go up. They were worried about me. They kept telling me I needed to be on medication and at one point I did take the medication, out of panic, but after a night of pure hell when I experienced most of the side effects that come with this particular medication, I knew I would have to be the one to save myself. I decided I would only talk to people who believed I could heal myself. I knew the others meant well, but I also knew I needed to protect my thoughts and the energy that coursed through my body. My boundaries became stronger and more solid as I noticed the effects different people had on me.

I ended up deciding to stop seeing the woman who worked with Chinese medicine. I kept telling her it felt like I was taking too many supplements. She insisted I needed all of them to get better. She constantly looked worried and concerned for me, and I noticed I would leave each visit feeling more and more worried about myself. In subtle ways she would talk down to me, and I realized I needed to only be with healers who I felt lifted me up and encouraged me. My mental state was crucial to my healing, and I needed to protect it. The energy of the person helping us heal is incredibly important. How we feel around them affects our health and recovery tremendously. This goes for therapists, doctors, massage therapists, naturopathic doctors, chiropractors, every type of healer. It is imperative that we listen to our bodies when we are around these people. It is of the utmost importance that we feel seen, heard, and safe.

When we are in a vulnerable state, like I was, we need to surround ourselves with people who respect us, who listen to us, and around whom we feel comfortable and relaxed. It is easy to fall into the conditioned behavior of seeing any medical or naturopathic professional as the expert and give away our power to them. The truth is, no one knows your body more than you do.

In Ashland, I discovered another woman who helps people who have experienced a lot of trauma. The first time I saw her I had to lie down for our conversation. Sitting up was too much for me at the time. My energy was at an all-time low. She had a big heart, and I could feel she really cared about me. She was very concerned at the state I was in. She told me my health wasn't stable enough for her treatments, that I should keep doing what I was doing to heal and come back in a couple weeks. I found her through an internet search after discovering something called *IASIS micro current neurofeedback*. The reviews and testimonials sounded amazing. This is a process where, as she explained it to me, a machine sends a signal to your brain to help it see what it needs to do to heal, and your body then learns and takes action to correct things. It is known to help with PTSD and Complex PTSD. I had many of the symptoms of both. Supposedly it is also effective at releasing trauma from the body, helping with sleep, anxiety, and depression. I watched many video testimonials about how it had dramatically helped others and was excited to begin treatments.

During this healing period I decided to begin each morning reciting positive affirmations about my body and its ability to heal itself. I listened to calming music. I juiced celery every morning, and ate lots of fresh fruits and vegetables, staying away from things like sugar, white flour, and other foods that would be harder for my body to digest. I ate foods to cleanse my liver and fill my body with healing nutrients. I made sure to be in nature every day. I sat out on the balcony of my condo, curled up in my papasan chair with a blanket over me, and would watch the birds or listen to relaxing music to help bring me calm.

When I was able to sit up for more than 30 minutes, I went for my first IASIS treatment. The practitioner put it on the lowest possible setting for me, knowing how sensitive my body was. I felt emotional after that session and found myself crying a lot. She said that was part of the trauma releasing, so I let myself cry. I cradled myself in that papasan chair every day. After the second and third session I felt progressively worse and sank into a deep depression. My son became very worried about me and told me he didn't feel good about these treatments. He explained the difference he had seen in me since starting the protocol. I told the facilitator, and she became concerned. She said she had always kept it at a low setting and had never seen a reaction like this before. I couldn't stop crying for a week straight. It was too much for my tender body. My health began to decline even more. She recommended we do a stronger treatment. In my weakened and frightened state, I had a moment of strength, and said, "No. I'm done. I don't want any more sessions. This is too much for my body."

I went home, concerned about myself, but also feeling fiercely protective of my body. I had been through so much for so long. I only wanted to feel good from now on. I knew more than ever what a vulnerable place I was in and I only wanted to receive treatment that helped and modalities that felt good to me and built me up, provided only by people with whom I felt completely comfortable and safe.

I decided then and there to let go of all the healers I had stacked my schedule with, except for one—Alaya, the Five Element acupuncturist. She was different from all the rest. She was calming, kind, and empowering. She would begin each session asking me how I was and what I felt my body and heart wanted that day. This is exactly what I needed. I felt safe, respected, and listened to, and I felt relief after every session. The environment we were in helped too. We met in an enclosed wooden gazebo in the backyard of a home. I would lie on her comfy massage table. She would drape cozy blankets over me, and I would look up at a large redwood tree, while listening to calming music playing in the background. Her voice was gentle and soothing. She treated me with empathy and compassion and had complete confidence in my body's ability to heal. She would begin by listening to my pulses. She could tell from that how my liver was doing, my kidneys, and other organs in my body. I love how this modality aids the body in healing itself. It deals with the underlying causes of a disease and helps restore the overall balance of your energy.

She would then place needles in areas of my body where energy was blocked and needed to be released. I felt my body settle down with each treatment, and some would bring me incredible peace. I would go home, once again curl up in my papasan chair, and sink into that peaceful state, staying there as long as I possibly could. For me it felt like it would bring my body to a place where it would experience how it was meant to feel, how it was designed to feel. I felt like my body had gotten so used to feeling anxiety, fear, sadness, and grief, it needed to be reminded of how life was meant to be. I think we, as humans, have strayed so far from how life is really supposed to be experienced.

What was amazing about my time with Alaya was that she had decided to close her practice and work on other passion projects, but when I reached out to her over the phone, she intuitively felt she needed to help me. I was her one and only client. I do believe we are not alone in this world, and even though I have experienced so much hurt and pain from people here, I have also felt carried and held and cared for. When we pursue healing, life helps us along our path and brings the right people into our lives. I was so humbled and deeply moved by this act of love by Alaya for me. I felt the sense that I was being watched over and would always be taken care of by true and pure love.

Alaya and I also had wonderful conversations about life. I've always had this innate knowing inside me of how life is supposed to be, how it is supposed to feel. She would talk about the flow of life. We talked about how we aren't designed to go, go, go, but rather to flow with the seasons and rhythms of life. I knew I needed and wanted to learn a new way of being here and the key was listening, being, observing. She kept encouraging me to go with the season of winter we were in and rest, really rest. Be with myself. Allow the emotions to come and simply be with them.

I knew my body needed to get back to its original state, to its homeostasis, which I believe is peace and harmony. I spent many days just being in that papasan chair, watching birds and trees sway in the wind, and spending time by the lake. Water calms me. I spent a lot of time alone, cocooning. I could feel the symptoms of high blood pressure leaving me more and more each day. My body was calming down. I was connecting with how life is supposed to feel. I had many moments in nature where I felt deep, profound peace like never before.

When we live with narcissists, we lose touch with how our bodies are meant to feel. In fact, we are thrown out of our bodies daily, because if we were to be present with everything we are feeling, it would be too much to handle. We are designed for love, for kindness, for harmony. We were never meant to experience abuse—it goes against everything we are designed for.

CHAPTER EIGHT

Trauma and the Nervous System

"Trauma fundamentally means a disconnection from self.
Why do we get disconnected?
Because it is too painful to be ourselves."

– Dr. Gabor Maté, *The Wisdom of Trauma* documentary

EVENTUALLY I STOPPED GOING TO ALAYA. I reached a point where I felt I had received what I needed and I wanted to take it from there, on my own, listening to myself and giving my body what it needed.

Gradually I felt better and my blood pressure lowered, but then other health issues began cropping up. I broke out in a rash all over my body. One morning I noticed a lump on my breast. Massive fear would rush through me with each issue that appeared, but then with time, a confidence would rise. I would lie down and listen to my body. "What do you need?" I would ask it. I had a growing conviction that my body knew how to heal itself, and I just needed to slow down and listen to its guidance. In every case, I was led to things I could do that would eventually dissipate all symptoms. My body was teaching me, and for the first time in my life I was listening more intently than ever.

After months of eating well and listening to my body, I wondered why I was still so anxious, why the muscles in my body felt constantly tight, why I still wasn't sleeping well, and still found myself jumpy and reactive. I began reading more about the effects of ongoing trauma on the nervous system. After reading a lot and watching many videos

I became intrigued by how the autonomic nervous system works. I saw links to symptoms I was having and had experienced for years. I signed up for a course on the subject because I was beginning to realize how important this information is for healing after narcissistic abuse. I'm excited to share with you what I learned and the exercises I now practice daily, which have made a huge difference in restoring my body, mind, and heart.

When you experience narcissistic abuse over months, years, or decades, your nervous system is greatly affected. Chronic abuse, which is the reality of what you have experienced, is trauma to the body. It is an important part of healing to recognize that what you experienced was indeed abuse, and all abuse is trauma to the body.

Our bodies are amazing and work hard to protect us, to keep us alive. They are designed to handle periodic stressors that happen in life. The problem comes when the stress in our lives is constant and ongoing, as it is when we live or work with a narcissist.

When our nervous system is working as it is meant to, we experience a natural progression of heightened reactions, followed by a calming down. For example, when you are driving in traffic and you see the car in front of you suddenly slam on their brakes, your sympathetic nervous system kicks in. In a split-second your body reacts before you have a chance to think and process. You quickly slam on your brakes or veer off to the shoulder to avoid an accident. You might stop on the side of the road to catch your breath. You can feel heightened energy and awareness surging through your body. Your breathing is faster. Your heart starts beating more rapidly. Your body might start shaking. Then slowly you feel things calming down inside you. You feel you are ready to get back into the flow of traffic. When you get home you sit or lie down and your body gradually and gently comes back to homeostasis. All is well. The stressful event is behind you and now you can move on with your life. That is the rhythm of a healthy, regulated autonomic nervous system.

If you have lived or worked with a narcissist, you have experienced stress on a daily and consistent basis. You probably felt like you were walking on eggshells around them, feeling their ever-changing moods permeate the air. Around them, you felt as if you were never good enough, always a disappointment. You experienced the exhausting and confusing intermittent reinforcement of sometimes receiving morsels of love, only to be followed by subtle or overt demeaning messages about yourself. Life with a narcissist is living in a state of constant stress and anxiety. Over time this ends up being too much for the body. What happens to our nervous system is it goes into states of flight, fight, or freeze to survive. Our system becomes dysregulated. We become reactive people. The smallest stressors feel like too much. Something goes wrong in our day, and we have a reaction to it that is stronger than normal. Emotions run high. We feel unstable. The world feels like too much to handle. Our environment feels unsafe. Sometimes we feel frozen inside, numb. Or we feel angry and anxious all the time, knowing this isn't really who we are. We spike into high levels of anxiety and then crash into low places of depression, despair, and hopelessness. We feel all over the place emotionally. We know this isn't who we really are, but we have no idea how to change what we're feeling.

When your nervous system is dysregulated you can feel like you are always "on." Like you are on alert all the time. You feel like your muscles are constantly tight. It's as if you are prey in the wild, always aware that a lion or another predator could leap out at any minute. After time your body doesn't know how to come down naturally. It is not meant to feel constant fear, stress, and anxiety. As a result, all the systems in your body are affected. This is one reason those of us who have experienced this for so many years end up having health issues. When the nervous system becomes dysregulated, our digestive system is affected, as well as our immune system, muscular system, cardiovascular system, and brain function. It feels like our thinking isn't clear, but foggy.

When your body has been in a relationship where you feel unsafe 24 hours a day, seven days a week, it reacts. This knowing can be either conscious or subconscious. If you are with an overt narcissist the feeling of being unsafe will be apparent. If you are with a covert narcissist, you will not be aware that you are in an unsafe environment, but your body will know and will feel it, often without you being aware until years later.

The good news is our bodies are designed to heal, and we are capable of restoring our nervous system.

When we experience chronic trauma and stress we get pulled out of the present, the here and now, because what we are feeling is too much. It's too overwhelming. As a result, we begin to disconnect from our bodies and the world around us because both of those places feel unsafe. The way to regulate your autonomic nervous system is to create safety and presence, to give your mind and body the message that everything in this moment is okay, and that you are safe.

This is not an overnight process. It will take time, but the results will amaze you. I'm going to share with you some exercises and practices I've learned and practice daily that have made a huge difference in the way I feel and experience life. The great news is they are all simple, don't cost anything, and don't take up much time. The key is consistency.

Before I explain the exercises, I want to let you know the difference they have made for me, to give you hope and demonstrate the power of these easy and gentle exercises.

Since I have implemented these exercises in my life, I have seen a tremendous difference in how I feel and operate. My body feels calmer, more settled down. I don't get as rattled by small stressors that come up. There is a steadiness I feel inside me, a quiet reassurance. After years of waking up throughout the night, my sleep has become more regular. I have more of an intimate connection with my body, where I'm able to notice how it feels in each moment, how it responds to things and ideas. This also results in me being able to see through others' manipulative behaviors more easily. Regulating your nervous system will actually safeguard you from predatory people. You will recognize toxic behavior more quickly.

I find I trust life more and move through fears that come up in me more easily. My emotions are less all over the place, and more stable the more I do the exercises. There is a peace that settles into my body more often. The love I have for myself and others has increased.

I am less reactive than I used to be. I take my time responding to people and making decisions.

I don't have as many traumatic flashbacks as I used to, and if I do, I now know how to hold myself through them, and reassure my body that we are safe now.

There is a relationship that I am fostering with myself and with life that feels very sweet, tender, and strong.

I also notice that when I go long periods of time without incorporating these exercises, some Complex PTSD symptoms begin to return—more anxiety and fear, interrupted sleep, and the feeling of being disconnected with my body and life. As soon as I once again make them a habit, I feel my body settling down and my nervous system regulating again.

As I mentioned before, this is not an overnight change, this is a new way of being with yourself and the world around you.

I gathered these practices from various books and articles I read about trauma and the nervous system.

The first one I learned from Dr. Peter A. Levine, one of my favorite authors on this subject. I highly recommend any of his books. There is so much information about this topic, and I am certainly not an expert. I won't cover all there is to say about regulating the nervous system here, so if you would like to research more, I have a list of books on this topic that I recommend at the end of this book.

Here are the exercises I do that have helped me regulate my nervous system:

1. This is My Hand, This is My Body

Place your hand on top of your other hand, and say, "This is my hand. This is my body." Then move on to other body parts. For instance, place your hand on your leg and say, "This is my leg, this is my body," then place your hand gently on your shoulder and say, "This is my shoulder, this is my body." Keep going with this as long as you like. Whenever I do this, I feel an immediate settling within me. There is something about the simplicity of acknowledging your body that helps you feel safe. It also helps connect you with the gorgeous vehicle you live in, and ushers you into the present moment.

I used to wake up feeling panicked and fearful. I started to implement this exercise the minute I woke up by immediately turning onto my side, holding my hand, and saying the words, "This is my hand, this is my body." It would help orient my body in safety and ended up becoming part of my morning ritual. I felt so safe lying there in bed as my body settled down. It felt so loving and gentle. It is a wonderful way to begin your day; feeling safe, letting your body know it is safe, sets the tone for the rest of your day.

I also do this when I am in a room with people and begin to feel anxious. I will place my hand on my leg and in my mind say the words, "This is my leg, this is my body." I will also do this when I find myself talking to someone around whom I don't feel safe, but for whatever reason need to converse with briefly. I'll do it in ways they don't notice. For example, if I am standing there listening to them talk, I will place my hand in a position that looks natural and say the words in my mind. It settles me down and feels reassuring. It also feels incredibly loving and caretaking. It is more proof to your body and your tender heart that you will take care of them, and this will help you build trust with yourself over time.

2. Noticing Your Environment

When we experience years of trauma, the world, the environment we live in, ends up feeling unsafe to us. An exercise that helps us feel safe again in our environment is to take time to notice objects around you. This can be done anywhere. You can lie in your bed as you wake up and slowly notice things around you. Take your time with this. These are all exercises that are meant to feel gentle.

You might look at your window. Notice the ledge under the window if you have one in your room. Notice the light fixture on the ceiling, or a lamp nearby. Gaze at the light switch on the wall. Look down at the floors and notice what they look like. Notice the sheets you are lying on.

I love doing this outside. Noticing each tree, each leaf, the trunk of the tree. Gazing at the clouds, maybe watching a bird come by. Looking at a rock, noticing the details of it.

I've also developed a habit of doing this in my car. When I first sit down in the driver's seat, before I start the engine, I will take a minute to look at the steering wheel, to notice the dashboard, and to glance at the knobs by the radio.

Doing this helps orient you to your surroundings, and like all the exercises, the more you do it the more you will feel your body settling down, because it is learning that it is safe exactly where it is. There is nothing to fear in this moment. All is well.

3. Connect Your Body with Your Environment

This exercise can be done while standing, walking, sitting, or lying down. The idea is to notice how it feels for your body to interact with different objects in your environment. This helps bring a feeling of connection, awareness, presence, and safety to your body.

If you are sitting right now, notice how your legs feel against the surface of the object it is sitting on. I do this the moment I sit in my car. Before I turn on the engine, I pay attention to my hands on the steering wheel, noticing how the texture feels touching them. I notice how my legs feel on the seat and my feet feel in my shoes, touching the pedals.

This can be done while you are working on the computer, as you are typing. Take a moment to notice how your fingers feel as they dance around the keyboard. I love how this exercise also brings in the wonder of how amazing our bodies are. As I do this practice I feel a deep love and appreciation for my body.

You can pay attention to how your feet feel touching the floor when you first get out of bed in the morning. Then notice each movement as you walk slowly around your room. Observe your hand as it circles a glass of water, holding it perfectly, and how the glass feels as it gently touches your lips.

You can do this for as long as you'd like, or just spend a couple minutes here and there throughout the day. The same can be said for the previous two exercises above. Any moment of focusing attention on your body and your environment will contribute to bringing your nervous system back into a regulated state.

To help make this easy and relaxing, I have created a guided meditation that walks you through this exercise. It can be found on my website and is mentioned in the resource page at the end of this book.

4. Honor Your Natural Impulses

After living or working with a narcissist you have most likely learned to ignore your own needs, feelings, and desires in exchange for making the narcissist the center of attention. That is the only way they would have stayed with you. The minute you begin to become stronger and pursue things that light you up is the moment the relationship no longer works for them and they no longer want or need you in their life.

Putting our attention on others and ignoring our own needs and desires also contributes to a dysregulated nervous system. Many of us were raised to believe this was an honorable way to live, pouring out our life-force energy to help others, while ignoring our own needs. In the long run this can lead to health issues. We are not made to live that way. Life is a balance of giving and receiving. A key to learning that balance is to begin the practice of listening to and honoring our body's natural impulses.

The body we live in is amazing. It knows exactly what it needs in each moment. The important thing for us is to learn to listen and pay attention to it. Acting on our natural impulses helps our autonomic nervous system and builds trust and safety within us.

This can be simple things such as, if you feel you need to go to the restroom, honor that. Don't wait. Go if you need to go. If you are thirsty, get yourself some water. This sounds obvious, but there are so many times we delay these needs throughout our day. Many of us have learned to "push through" these impulses to get things done. We let other things take precedence. If you are hungry, eat. Tired? Lie down. If you feel the need to move, take a quick or long walk, or stretch, or dance. Whatever type of movement would feel good to you.

When I am feeling restless or emotional or unsettled, or some other uncomfortable or confusing state of being, I will stop and ask my body what it needs, what would feel good to it right then. Does it want to move, go outside, eat, sleep, talk to a friend, cry, dance, listen to music?

Sometimes I don't know what I need. At those times, I lie down or sit down until it's clear to me. I stay with my body and listen and notice. This happened just minutes ago, in fact. I sat down to type out this section of the book and for some reason nothing was coming. I tried to push myself to write and typed various things, but none of it felt right. I kept deleting sentences. I've learned this is my signal to stop writing and see what my body needs. I laid down and tried to feel into what I needed. Was I tired? Did my body want to take a walk outside? Did I need to feel something? After a few minutes of not being clear I began to cry. Flashes came to my mind of the previous couple of days and some news I had received concerning someone I care about, and a hurtful conversation with a family member. As the memories came to mind the tears turned into deeper crying. I let them flow. I allowed myself to feel whatever came up, realizing that was what I needed. Once I felt complete, I opened my laptop and the words flowed out of me with ease.

You'll find the more you do this, a sweet and beautiful relationship with yourself will arise. If you are someone who leans toward perfectionism, please know this is not about doing things right and perfect. This is about being tender with yourself, being there for your heart and body. It won't always be clear what you need, but just asking yourself what you need and desire and crave is a powerful beginning. It is establishing a new habit and a new way of being there for yourself.

5. Feel Your Feelings

The fifth exercise that will help your nervous system is all about emotions. If you were raised by a narcissist or in a long-term relationship with one, you most likely received the message that your feelings did not matter, only theirs did. This could not be further from the truth. Your feelings matter, always. Your heart matters. Every emotion you feel is important and needs to be felt and expressed. Our bodies are made to feel, not suppress.

Many of us were raised in environments that did not encourage the free expression of emotions. For some of us, we received the message that some emotions were shameful and bad. Maybe you were taught that you need to be grateful and positive all the time. If you were not content, you were being selfish and entitled. When you felt strong emotions maybe you were told you need to change your attitude. There are so many unhealthy beliefs about emotions and it is important that we learn that feeling emotions is normal, natural, and part of being human. There are no good or bad emotions. It's all energy, and we need to learn how to be with each one in a healthy way.

I have spoken to many people who are afraid to be angry, because they watched their father or mother get angry and yell at them or at the other parent. They saw the hurt and destruction anger can cause when expressed in an unhealthy and cruel way. It is important to know there is a place for anger. It just needs to be expressed in a way where no one gets hurt.

Part of learning to love yourself is learning to accept everything you feel, with no judgment. The truth is emotions are simply waves of energy passing through your body. Because of our conditioning we can become fearful when the waves come. If we feel sad or depressed, we can wonder if something is wrong with us. If we feel numb or hopeless, we can begin to fear that we might always feel this way. These thoughts intensify and prolong the emotions. But if we accept that we are emotional beings, we can learn to acknowledge each wave and be with it, flow with it, and learn to listen to what our body needs. We need to become compassionate listeners.

Let's look at a few emotions that arise in us.

Anger is a fantastic emotion that can fuel us to protect those we love. It can make us move mountains, change laws, seek justice, and make this world a better place.

Sadness is such a tender emotion. I've learned to hold myself so gently when I feel sad and treat myself in ways that are calming and caretaking.

Grief is a deep feeling and is common after these types of relationships. Similar to sadness, with grief I've learned to let myself stay there as long as I need to, and cry for as long as I need to. I love myself tenderly here, letting myself know how sorry I am for what

I've experienced. I hold myself like a loving friend would, and I give myself space to grieve. I think grief and sadness can bring us into presence in a beautiful way. And when grief has passed, I feel extra gratitude for people who love me well, for the sunset, for the birds, for the trees, the flowers, cozy blankets, music, and all the other things that add so much richness and beauty to our lives. Grief, if allowed to be felt, can bring us into a place of deep gratitude.

There is no need to fear emotions. They can't hurt us. The more we learn to accept their existence and ride each wave with compassion, the less the uncomfortable ones tend to show up.

CHAPTER NINE

Did They Ever Really Love You?

W HEN YOU REALIZE THE PERSON YOU WERE WITH, or were raised by, is a narcissist, it is common and natural to wonder if they ever really loved you. Was it all a lie? Was any part of it love? This is an aspect of cognitive dissonance that is so difficult to deal with, and the more covert they were, the harder it can be. You run through all the memories in your mind. I'm sure there were times you received kind notes, messages, emails, and cards. Maybe they would tell others how great you are. They may have given you gifts from time to time. There were laughs and good times mixed in with the devaluing, controlling, and manipulative behavior. You truly loved them and thought you felt the same from them. What was the truth? Did they really love you, or did they just mirror the love and enthusiasm that was coming from you?

There could have been moments where they felt love for you. The important thing is to look at your overall experience and ask yourself, *Could the treatment I received have come from love?*

There may have been real emotions at the beginning, but feelings can shift and change. Not love, however. Love is consistent.

The truth is narcissists have a lust for power and control, and they look for people who are weak in areas they can exploit. The perfect person for a narcissist is someone who does not have a clear picture and experience of love, someone who is kind, giving, nurturing, and doesn't have strong boundaries. This person is a gold mine for them.

That's why you may have noticed that things started falling apart in the relationship when you began to become strong, when you set boundaries, and when you began to question how they were treating you. When this happens, they no longer needed or wanted you in their life.

You were chosen to play a role you didn't know you auditioned for at the very beginning.

When you stop playing the role you were assigned, they discard you, and almost immediately begin auditioning others for their next casting. You aren't replaced, really. The role you were cast in gets replaced. I hope that realization brings you comfort and relief. It is such a painful experience when we are brutally discarded. You might be asking yourself, *How was I so easily replaced?* You weren't. Your role was.

From my research and experience, I believe narcissists are filled with deep internal fear and as a result they don't allow themselves to fully trust others. They choose to control people rather than risk vulnerability and real connection. Because of this it is impossible for them to experience deep, fulfilling relationships. Ironically the narcissistic choices they make based on their deep fears and lust for power end up making them their own self-created and self-inflicted victim. Unless they choose to change, they will never be able to experience the full joy of life, the healing river of love, and the calming stillness of peace.

Understanding why someone is a narcissist does not mean you need to save or rescue them from their hidden fears. Only they can change themselves. No amount of your love will help anyone change or heal unless they want that themselves. There are many people on this planet who are filled with loving, genuine, trusting hearts. Narcissists have ample opportunity to heal and experience love, but it is up to them to make that choice. It is up to them to want to heal and to seek that healing. No one else can do this for them.

When someone chooses to be narcissistic, they become incapable of loving others. For someone to really love someone else they must have empathy and compassion and narcissists do not have either.

When someone chooses power and control over love, it lets us know what is going on inside them. If they were filled with love, they would have no desire for control. The more each of us fills ourselves with love, the more we trust and flow with life. When we are in this state, the thought of controlling anyone or anything is far from our consciousness.

You have probably noticed that the more you treat yourself with love, the more loving you find yourself being to those around you. This lets you know what is going on inside a narcissist. When you feel their hatred and rage toward you, it's a reflection of the rage and hatred they have toward themselves.

Ultimately, we all treat others the way we see and treat ourselves. Someone who is filled with love would never devalue or demean someone else. The two cannot exist at the same time. Where there is love, there can never be cruelty.

Do I believe narcissists can change? Absolutely. Each of us has free will and the ability to heal and change. I believe everyone is capable of love. We are all made for love, to be loved, and to love others and ourselves. What path we choose is up to each of us. No one can choose for us. In order to change, a narcissist must want to change. No amount of your love will change them. It must come from inside of them.

Love also never creates confusion. When you are around love, you feel wanted, desired, and valued. Love would never dream of saying or doing anything to devalue you. Love doesn't control or manipulate. When you are in the presence of true love, you feel as if you can exhale because you know your full self is welcome and wanted. Love—authentic, real love—is unconditional. It is filled with grace and gentleness. It feels healing, soothing, and empowering. It is caretaking, nurturing, and consistent.

There is never any cognitive dissonance where love prevails. There is peace, harmony, and kindness.

My guess is that you did not experience this with the narcissist in your life. They may have had moments where they felt love when they were around you, but overall, they were not coming from a place of true, life-giving, real love.

CHAPTER TEN

Forgiving Yourself for Not Seeing

MANY PEOPLE WHO HAVE BEEN IN A RELATIONSHIP with a narcissist have a difficult time forgiving themselves for not seeing through the lies and manipulation. "How could I have not seen this? How could I have lived with this person for so long and not noticed? I am smart. I am intuitive. I usually see through people." These are questions and comments I hear a lot from survivors.

If these are thoughts you have had or are having, know that I have talked to many licensed therapists who know all about narcissism, who have counseled people for decades, and who still were not able to recognize the covert manipulation they experienced for years in their own life.

The more covert the narcissist is, the harder it is to see through their behavior. We also need to keep in mind that even if they were more overt, if we experienced that behavior growing up, we won't see it as unhealthy and cruel, we will view it as normal.

The fact that you were not able to see through the behavior is not your fault, and one of the most important things your heart needs after this type of abuse is grace.

The Merriam-Webster dictionary uses some beautiful and healing words to define grace—as mercy, pardon, an act of kindness, and courtesy. This is what you need and deserve. Really take those words in for a moment. Mercy. Pardon. Kindness. Not only the feeling of the word *kindness*, but the act of kindness. Let your words and actions toward yourself express kindness.

You have been through an incredible experience. The manipulation narcissists use is masterful and so difficult to see through.

A narcissist will use your deepest wounds to control and manipulate you. They also use your greatest gifts and your generous heart against you. That type of manipulation is difficult to recognize.

So many of us have had our hearts trampled in ways that are difficult to see. We are not designed to be treated in deceptive ways, to be used and then discarded. This behavior is cruel and it takes time to heal.

Give yourself time. Give yourself grace. The manipulation you experienced was not your fault. You did not deserve it. And millions upon millions of people around the world don't see through the lies, manipulation, and control. You are not alone. In fact, you are in the company of some wonderful people like yourself with big hearts, a propensity to love, to help others, and to lift others up. We did not know there was a whole tribe of us out there living through the same things. When we find each other, we feel we can exhale.

Hold your heart tenderly through this healing process and tell yourself often that it is completely understandable that you did not see clearly when you were in this relationship, and that it will take time to unravel the truth, and that's okay. You are going to be okay. You are learning important information that will change you and bring you tremendous freedom and strength.

Leaving a relationship with a narcissist really is like coming out of a cult. There is a lot of deprogramming to do, along with rebuilding. The good news is, full healing is possible, and you are worth the time and effort. You deserve to heal. Your body deserves to feel good. And you deserve to bathe in grace for the rest of your beautiful life.

CHAPTER ELEVEN

Why Narcissists Behave the Way They Do

L ET'S LOOK IN MORE DETAIL AT WHY NARCISSISTS BEHAVE the way they do. There are many contributing factors. They are insecure, filled with fear and rage, have unresolved issues, are full of self-hatred, and have a lust for power. Some of them were raised in abusive homes, while others were raised in homes where they were trained to be entitled and see themselves as more special than others. Many were raised to see others as only being here to serve them. They are self-centered and have no interest in harmonious relationships. Ultimately, they are out for themselves and put their desires and needs before others. They are lost inside and far away from who they really are.

This is their choice, and it is important to realize that. No one is forcing them to be cruel and selfish. They can choose to heal. They can choose to find help. Everyone has free will. I mentioned this earlier, but it bears repeating because I have heard from so many targets who believe they can rescue the narcissist. It's an important lesson for survivors to learn that we cannot save them. We cannot help anyone who does not want to heal themselves.

It is common for people who are with narcissists to think, *If I had just loved them more, been more compassionate, listened more, maybe they would have changed.*

We can only change ourselves. We are all on our own paths, with our own journeys to experience, and only we can learn the lessons we need and want to. This is our work, and they have theirs. As we heal, it is helpful to learn to stay in our own lane.

It is also important after we leave a narcissist to surround ourselves with others who give us freedom to be ourselves, safety to open our hearts, and love to remind us of who we are and how we are meant to experience life.

There is a lot that can be said about why narcissists abuse, but in this chapter, I will explain two of the reasons I personally have come to believe from my own observations and conversations with others in the mental health field. These two reasons often go unnoticed, but I believe are important to be aware of for your own healing and understanding. Being able to recognize them will help you make sense of the way you have been treated, and, I hope, bring you relief as you realize it had nothing to do with you.

Anyone who has been with a narcissist knows the feeling of their rage. If they were overt, you would see and hear their rage, you would experience them yelling, calling you names, putting you down, and possibly physically harming you. If they were covert, the rage was more hidden. It comes out in more passive-aggressive ways like the silent treatment and punishing you in ways that can't be traced back to them, or in subtle ways that cause you to give them the benefit of the doubt. With the covert type you can feel the hidden rage inside them. It permeates the air and makes you feel like you have to walk on eggshells.

Their rage is often directed at you. You can feel them despising you, hating you, and you can't figure out why. It makes you wonder if you really are awful to live with and your behaviors are the cause of their anger. Some will tell you that outright, and others will imply it. I believe this hostility toward you is rage inside them that is misplaced. This misplaced rage is the first reason for their behavior that I want to make you aware of.

Think about the narcissist in your life. What was their relationship with their mother or father like? Or sibling? Usually there was some way they were mistreated growing up. Instead of being honest about how hurt they were or angry they are now as an adult, instead of facing that sorrow and pain and seeking help and healing, they choose to take it out on others. They use other people as targets for the rage that is unconsciously meant for someone else. Many of us do this in small ways, but for a narcissist this becomes a lifestyle.

In some cases, covert narcissists were treated terribly by a parent. They may tell you they've forgiven them and all is good now. Or they may tell you they choose to think positively and don't want to focus on the negative. You might react by thinking, *Really? Wow. You're a better person than I am. It would take a lot for me to get over the way they treated you.* The truth is they are bypassing the pain and anger they feel toward that parent. They haven't dealt with their experience in an honest way, and since our feelings must go somewhere, they direct their rage at you. You are essentially the scapegoat for their resentment toward someone else.

You are not actually the source of their rage. I hope you can see this. You have nothing to do with their rage. You did not cause them to feel rage. This is an internal issue that they are choosing not to deal with.

The second reason I believe narcissists behave the way they do is that they are deeply unhappy about certain things in their life, and because they are unhappy, in their minds, you are also not allowed to be happy. If they can't be happy, no one can. I am sure you have noticed anytime you are feeling good, or pursuing something you are excited about, such as going on a trip that brings you joy, they will try to somehow sabotage your joy and light. Often what they focus on in you relates specifically to the source of their own unhappiness. This takes some unpacking and looking beneath the surface to see.

Think about the main things they put you down for or said are wrong with you. Before I explain further, write those things down in the space below. Later, after I explain how their messages are linked to the narcissist's own unhappiness, you can come back to your answers and see them from a different perspective.

Let's say, as an example, they say or imply that you are lazy. They tell you that you should be working harder, that life isn't going to come easy. "You must work hard in this life," is their anthem. "You shouldn't rely on anyone to help you. Your dreams are foolish and not practical. You want everything to come easily for you. Well, that's not how the world works. Unless you are working 40-plus hours a week at a job you don't like, you are lazy."

They repeat this message over and over. You end up believing that you are lazy, that your dream of being an artist, a writer, a singer, a painter, a digital nomad, a dancer, or a photographer is foolish and unrealistic. You feel disempowered and discouraged. You take a job that doesn't feed your soul and ends up draining you because you resign yourself to a life centered around paying bills and trying to save as much money as possible. Your energy and light dim over time and you slowly bury your dreams.

Here is the truth of this scenario. Somewhere in the narcissist's life, they buried their own dreams. They took a path that didn't light them up. They aren't happy with their own job, and being a narcissist, if they aren't happy, they are going to darn well make sure that you are not happy. Anytime you decide to go in the direction of a career that brings you joy, they will try to shut that down. If they believe they can't make money doing the things they really want to do, if they deep down wish their life was easier, and they didn't have to work so hard doing things they don't enjoy, then you are not allowed to have that either. Anytime you feel joyful about something, it triggers their jealousy and this unconsciously reminds them of their own unhappiness. They don't want to live life feeling their honest feelings and facing their honest thoughts, so instead, they choose to punish you for the disappointment and hatred they feel for themselves and toward life.

Let's say you decide to figure out how you can pursue your dream and support yourself doing so. Let's say you dream of being a photographer, and you end up building a life where you can travel the world taking photos and working only 20 hours a week. Or maybe you love doing makeup and you're good at it, so you bravely start a YouTube channel and do makeup tutorials. Your channel gets popular, and you end up making more money than you thought possible doing something that is pure fun to you.

If the narcissist in your life has been preaching how life should look to you and sees the life you are living now, their narcissistic rage will be triggered. If they can't live their life the way they deep down want to, they won't be able to stand seeing you thriving and living life on your terms.

The life you naturally have inside you, your bright light that exists within you, is a reminder to them of what they don't have. Instead of being brave and admitting this, they choose to punish you for making them feel it.

Whatever they believe they were denied in life, they will speak about loudest.

It is reminiscent of the classic example of a religious leader who preaches loudly and often against gay people. Then years later we find out he has been hiring gay prostitutes for decades. He hated gay people because they were free to live the life they wanted, to be their true selves. He raged against them, because they reminded him of a place in his life where he was not free. Since he was not free to live the way he wanted to, he would make sure they couldn't either. This is an example of both misplaced rage and, "If I can't have what I want, then you can't either."

Whatever a narcissist preaches about most loudly and most often is linked to the parts of themselves they don't feel free to live out.

This is something for you to ponder if you would like to. Feel free to look back at how you answered the question in this chapter, and see if you can make any links between what the narcissist focuses on in you and unhappiness they might be experiencing in those same areas of their own life.

No narcissist is truly happy. None of them are thriving. It is impossible for narcissism and true happiness to exist in a person at the same time. People who are truly enjoying their life naturally want others to enjoy theirs too.

If the narcissist in your life acts as if their life is wonderful, don't believe it for a second. They are acting. You can always tell what is going on inside someone by the way they treat others.

You have experienced someone who has issues they have not dealt with and have instead used you as a target for their rage, hidden shame, and unhappiness.

I hope this realization brings you relief. I also hope it frees you to be your full self, and to live life the way you want to.

You know more than anyone what works best for you. You have all the answers you need inside you, and no one has the right to tell you how you should live your life.

CHAPTER TWELVE

Why Many Survivors Wonder if They are the Narcissist

I T IS COMMON FOR SURVIVORS TO WONDER if they are the narcissist. This happens for a few reasons.

One reason is sometimes a narcissist will tell you that you are a narcissist, or say you are being narcissistic. If they are covert, they will imply it or use other words to convey that message. Because you are a self-reflective person, you will look at yourself, you will spin your wheels and exhaust yourself trying to figure out if this is true about you. This is what the narcissist wants you to do. They want to exhaust you of your energy. This dynamic is one way they get energy from you and part of what makes you their energy supplier. They also want you to feel this confusion because it will distract you from seeing the truth about them. Another thing this does is minimize their abusive behavior by making it seem like you are just having a fight, calling each other names. You're both just hurt and angry and lashing out, like all couples. That is the narrative they want so they aren't exposed. This is gaslighting and makes you question yourself.

One thing to notice is that you are looking at yourself, wanting to make sure you are not being narcissistic, but do they ever look at themselves because they are so concerned they might be hurting you and being narcissistic? No, they don't. This is one of the many things that will tell you that you are not the narcissist. You care about other people's feelings and feel terrible if you think you might have hurt someone or treated them badly.

Another reason you can wonder if you are the narcissist is after being with one for so long, you have lost the confidence and ability to trust your own discernment and to see yourself clearly. You have become so used to giving your power away to the narcissist that it is easy to believe they know more than you do about who you are. Many narcissists will tell you that. They will tell you they know you better than you know yourself. No one knows you more than you do. You have been set up to doubt yourself. This is not your fault. It is a natural and understandable outcome of being in relationships with these energy vampires.

A third common reason you may wonder if you are the narcissist could relate to how you are defining narcissism. You may be seeing it as simply being selfish or self-focused. This is how many see narcissism until they really study the subject and realize how much more there is to it. You may feel like the focus is always on you when you talk to friends or family, since you are trying to sort out all that is going on in your life. Then you may wonder, *Am I narcissistic because everything is always about me?* When I was going through the discard phase, I felt incredibly self-focused for a long time. I felt like every conversation I had with my friends was centered around me. I feared draining them. I felt bad for always talking about myself. But here is the thing: I needed to. I needed them more than ever, and because they are loving, healthy people, they understood that. People who are emotionally mature know this is how life is. Healthy relationships are about giving and receiving. This was my time to receive. When I became stronger and they were going through their own painful things, it was my turn to give. This is the rhythm of life. You aren't being selfish. When you are in the midst of the greatest pain and confusion you've ever experienced, you need people more than ever. You won't always feel this way, but for now, allow yourself to be loved and cared for. You are worthy of that.

Another thing that happens that can cause us to see ourselves in a false light is that with the narcissist, we find ourselves behaving in ways that are not who we really are. We yell. We say things we are shocked came out of our mouths. We spy on them. We do things to get back at them. The reason this happens is that we are put in highly unusual situations, and that's what pushes us to do things we later regret and feel bad about. This adds to us wondering if we are really the one that is off, if we are really just as abusive as they are. The truth is we are having a natural reaction to abusive and crazy-making behavior. It is called crazy-making for a reason. It makes us act in ways that are not our typical way of behaving. This is a natural reaction to lies and accusations and gaslighting. We can feel like we are going crazy, like a wild animal who has been contained and abused for years and finally reacts and fights back. These are our natural instincts for how to react to the unnatural circumstances we are put in. It is important to see the difference between your occasional reactive behavior and the behavior of an actual narcissist, who emotionally and psychologically abuses people consistently for years and often decades with no remorse.

If you are wondering if you are a narcissist, answer these questions:

1. Do you demean and devalue people on a regular basis?
2. Do you gaslight people for the purpose of making them question their own reality?
3. Do you pit people against each other, as in the manipulation technique of triangulation?
4. Do you project your unresolved issues onto others?
5. Do you have rage inside you and use it to control others so they feel afraid and unsettled?
6. Do you manipulate others with your emotions on a regular basis?
7. When others are hurting, do you feel nothing? Do you lack empathy?

8. Are you arrogant? Do you believe rules don't apply to you like they do to others?

9. Do you lie on a regular basis?

10. In your relationships, do you say one thing and do another? Would your friends say your actions don't match your words?

If you answered yes to these questions, then I would say you have a chance of having narcissistic traits. But I have a feeling these behaviors do not describe you.

The fact that you are reading this book tells me you are not a narcissist. Narcissists are not interested in healing. The fact that you wonder if you are a narcissist tells me you probably aren't, because narcissists are not self-reflective. They do not wonder if they are a narcissist or see themselves as having issues.

I hope this chapter helps you see more clearly that you are not a narcissist or an abuser.

CHAPTER THIRTEEN

Why Do We End Up with Narcissists?

Many factors can contribute to why people unknowingly get into relationships with narcissists. One reason is we did not have a clear picture of what love looks like to begin with. So, we end up accepting behavior because it is familiar; it is similar to what we have experienced in the past.

Many of us repeat toxic patterns we learned in childhood. For instance, some people get the message that fighting is normal—they think it is a sign of passion and open communication. Some of us witnessed or learned that love looks like giving all of ourself in an unbalanced and unhealthy way to someone else, even if it costs us our health. Maybe this was seen as a virtue growing up. It was seen as loving. This type of thinking sets you up perfectly for a manipulative narcissist who wants to be the center of attention and looks for people who are already groomed to behave that way toward others.

Sometimes we have a parent who didn't take responsibility for their own issues and projected them onto us. We learned it was our job to accept responsibility for others in addition to ourselves. When we met the narcissist and they did the same thing, we unconsciously fell right into old patterns because we already knew this "dance." Emotionally healthy people would never want to put their issues onto you. But if you were taught the opposite from someone who raised you and treated you well in other ways, you learned to think of this behavior as normal. This is why self-love is so important—so you can build a new, accurate template of love within yourself that will enable you to see through the counterfeit.

The more you choose love in your own life, the more you will see that what you experienced with the narcissist was nowhere close to the real thing.

In addition to not having a clear example of what love looks like, many of us get into these relationships because we have not been taught or shown good boundaries. Maybe you were raised to always be kind, keep the peace, not ruffle any feathers. Many of us were not encouraged to stand up for ourselves when others are not treating us well.

Pleasing others might have been encouraged in our families, and things like looking out for yourself and self-care were viewed as selfish.

Some of us came from overtly abusive homes, others were raised by covertly abusive parents, and some of us had kind parents who lacked strength and healthy boundaries. For others, there was a mixture of kindness and abuse.

Growing up, many of us felt like we needed to be perfect, so when we met someone who required us to be perfect for them, it felt familiar to us. It felt normal.

Sometimes abuse that is familiar can feel subconsciously comforting. It feels like home, because that is what we equate with home.

Another aspect that contributes to us becoming prey is not having a relationship with ourselves where we trust our instincts, feelings, and bodily reactions. When we aren't connected with our body's signals, we become vulnerable to manipulation and gaslighting. Our bodies are incredibly smart. They are one of our most accurate barometers for truth. They will let us know if something is off, even if everything appears normal. When someone is lying to you, for instance, you will feel it in your body. If you don't have an awareness of this, you will let your mind talk you out of what your body is showing you. That is why it is so important to connect with and listen to your body.

Part of healing and safeguarding ourselves from getting into relationships with predators again is learning to develop a strong and trusting relationship with ourselves and our body, to relearn what love looks like, and to learn and implement healthy boundaries.

It is important to look at the reasons why we were okay with the treatment we received. This is also an important part of the healing process as it will help us have wisdom in future relationships.

Use the space below to explore insights that may have come up for you as you read this chapter. What do you think are some elements that could have contributed to you getting into a relationship with a narcissist? Were you encouraged to set boundaries growing up? Did you feel as if you needed to be perfect? Were you taught to stand up for yourself? Did you get the message you needed to please others no matter what you were feeling or how you were being treated? Was overlooking your own needs seen as a virtue?

CHAPTER FOURTEEN

Dating Again

AFTER BEING IN A RELATIONSHIP WITH A NARCISSIST, it is common and understandable to feel fear and hesitation when it comes to dating again, especially if you have been with a more covert type, or one who began covertly and became more overt over time. You have now seen that some abusers look and sound wonderful at first. They can be charming and tell you everything you long to hear. You may now wonder, *Who can I trust after believing someone who in the beginning appeared so kind, caring, and wonderful? Can I trust myself to see the traits of a narcissist this time? Will I end up with another one?*

It is important to realize that narcissists come in all shapes and sizes. There are different versions of the same thing. Because they can be difficult to recognize, it is important to move slowly and cautiously and pay close attention to your body. You have been through a traumatic experience and are vulnerable right now to people who prey on the wounded.

It is easy to get into a new relationship soon after a hurtful one ends because you are longing for love, craving someone to hold you, to see you, and to help build you up. However, during this time it is important to develop a strong relationship with yourself, to treat yourself with the love you long for before jumping into something with someone else. This will help you see clearly when you do begin dating again.

When you decide you are ready to date, it is important to be aware that many people who have been with an overt narcissist can get taken in by a covert narcissist. At first it feels so much better than what you experienced before, but after time you realize you are dealing with a different version of the same traits.

Covert types are the most hidden and so can appear to be the opposite of who they are. For example, I recently heard of a narcissist who is a life coach. His focus is on working with empaths. As you may know, empaths are perfect targets for narcissists and often end up in relationships with them. He creates programs specifically for empaths and ends up using them, confusing them, and draining them of their life-force energy. His clients become his energy source. The covert types can be humanitarians, spiritual leaders, therapists, and others who have learned how to act like they have empathy. Some will use their hardship stories to get you to give up your time, resources, and energy to help them.

Here is a list of some things to look out for and pay attention to as you begin to date again.

1. How is your energy when you are with this person, or after being around them?

If you find yourself feeling more and more depleted of energy, know that this is not a healthy sign. Even if you feel a lot of energy in the beginning, be sure this stays consistent over time. Think of people in your life who truly love you. They probably rarely drain you. If there are times they do, it is the exception rather than the rule. Healthy people who love you will affect your energy in a positive way. Healthy relationships don't deplete your life-force energy.

2. Is this a rescue mission?

Do you find yourself thinking and hoping that your love will change or "save" this person? Maybe they are going through difficult things and don't have love in their life, and you feel if you could be that love for them, they will be okay. You find yourself giving more than you are receiving. Over time you feel drained. You find them relying on you too much. They may say things like, "You are the only one who cares. I don't know what I would do without you." Know that you deserve to receive love just as much as you give it. Be with someone who is a whole person and actively works on themselves and takes responsibility for their own healing and growth. You should never feel that the other person would be helpless without you. Some covert narcissists use "poor me" stories to rope you in, because you are a naturally giving person. Your heart goes out to them, but they can end up using you and draining you.

3.   Do they have a lot of drama in their life?

Narcissists often create drama or attract it because it is an energy source for them. They also use it to get attention and to get you to feel sorry for them. They may even talk about how much they don't like drama to throw you off. Pay attention to how they live more than what they say. Be with someone who has the same values as you. If you value peace, harmony, and moving in the direction of a stable and drama-free life, be with someone who values these things as well and demonstrates this through their actions.

4.   Do you feel respected?

You deserve to be spoken to in a way that is and feels respectful— never talked down to, never belittled, and never demeaned. You also deserve to be with someone whose actions also show they respect you. There is never any reason for anyone to call you derogatory names. Be with someone who respects who you are, exactly the way you are right now.

5.   Do their actions match their words?

This sounds simple, but, as you know, after being with a narcissist, it is easy to miss. Pay close attention to their actions and see if they consistently match up with the words they say.

6. How does your body feel when you are with them?

Do you feel emotionally safe? Do you feel relaxed or tense? Do you feel free to be your full self? Or do you feel you need to be someone other than who you really are? When you communicate with them, is it easy for you to think clearly and express yourself honestly? Do you feel heard? Your body will let you know who this person is by how you feel.

7. How do you feel when you are intimate with them?

Do you feel pursued? Cherished? Beautiful? Handsome? Sexy? Do you feel like they want to give you pleasure? Or does it feel one-sided? Do you feel like you need to do all the work? Do you feel shamed in any way? Not good enough? The way someone treats you in bed reveals a lot about them. The way your body feels with them is a great barometer for the truth of who they are and how they will be as a partner.

8. Do you find yourself often giving them the benefit of the doubt and excusing their behavior?

When someone is emotionally healthy and genuinely loves you, you won't have to frequently give them the benefit of the doubt for their words or actions. You won't find yourself often excusing their behavior. Their love, words, and treatment of you will be consistent.

9. Do they seem vacant?

A healthy person will have a strong sense of self. When you look at them, can you see and feel a clear identity to them, or do they seem hollow? When they talk, do they feel like they are saying lines from a script? Is there a "smoothness" to them that doesn't feel real?

10. Do you feel free to be honest with them?

Do you find yourself watching what you say because you are afraid of how they may react? Do you feel like you have to walk on eggshells around them? Are their moods all over the place, and you never know what you are going to get? A healthy person will give you the consistent feeling that you can tell them anything that is on your heart or mind, because they really want to know. Your thoughts and feelings will matter to them.

If you are feeling fearful about starting over with someone else and possibly missing the signs, know that there is nothing to fear. Ultimately everything in life is an experience we can learn from. What we take from each one will help us grow and evolve. The key is to keep developing a loving relationship with yourself. The more you do that, the more you will become crystal clear on what love looks and feels like.

The great news is that because you had the courage and strength to leave a narcissist you now have a chance to experience real love. Settle for nothing less. This is what you deserve, and what you are designed to experience.

CHAPTER FIFTEEN

Smear Campaigns and Flying Monkeys

W HEN YOU LEAVE A NARCISSIST, one thing you will most likely experience are smear campaigns and the cruelty of their *flying monkeys*. This is a term used to describe people who are in their inner circle, who act on their behalf, usually for cruel and abusive purposes.

Flying monkeys' words and actions add to the confusion and cognitive dissonance we already have. They increase our belief of our unworthiness and our wonderings if things really are wrong with us. They minimize what we have been through and gaslight us into thinking it was not really abuse and that we are the one with the problem.

It is difficult and painful to know people are spreading misinformation about you, and to feel like there is nothing you can do about it. It is a helpless and disempowering feeling. And if you have children with the narcissist, seeing people trying to turn them against you is deeply painful.

The effects of the character attacks and the cruelty from the flying monkeys in my own life took its toll on my heart and body. After years of experiencing their venomous words and actions, I reached a point where I realized there was nothing I could do to change this reality. No matter what I did, no matter how good a person I was, they would probably always see me through the lens they were choosing to look through. It was painful, and it had a significant effect on both my mental and physical health. I came to the conclusion that the only way for me to survive, heal, and move on with my life was to somehow find a way to be okay with the lies that were being told about me. To somehow find a way to be okay with people seeing me as someone I wasn't.

When this thought came to me, I felt surprising hope. There was an internal shift within me. I realized I had a choice. The power was in my hands. I had gotten so used to feeling powerless. For so long, the narcissist in my life and the flying monkeys felt larger than life. It always felt like they had all the power. That's how bullies feel, and they are bullies.

When I came to the conclusion that I needed to find a way to be okay with other people believing lies about me, a strength grew in me. The realization that this was a possibility—that I could move forward in my life in spite of their words and actions—gave me my power back. I think when we get swallowed up in the helpless feeling of being overpowered, it seldom occurs to us that it is possible to reach a place where we are okay with it. It felt rebellious. It felt freeing. I had no idea how, but just accepting this as a possibility helped me.

I began to explore how I could be okay with all of it. I imagined what it would be like to accept everything in my life just the way it is. Whenever I sat with that, I felt relief in my body, an exhale. The more I sat with it, the more my body relaxed. This would be something I came back to again and again.

The behavior directed at me was not okay, but it was possible for me to be okay in the midst of it. The other key for me was the realization that this behavior—the cruelty and lies—was on them, the narcissist and the flying monkeys. Each of them was in charge of their behavior, how they chose to treat others. Essentially, none of it had anything to do with me. It was all theirs to own and deal with. I was only responsible for myself and my own choices about how I treated others.

One other thing I want to address with flying monkeys is how much they can make you doubt yourself. Something that helped me with this was to consider the things they would say to me and ask myself, "Would I ever say that to anyone else?"

Think of one cruel thing a flying monkey or a narcissist has told you about yourself. Would you ever say that to anyone else? My guess is you would not.

My own heart and conscience would never be okay with me uttering such callous words. Even after I have been hurt deeply by someone, I can't bring myself to say things I know would hurt them. For whatever reason, it is not in my DNA to treat others that way even when they have been horrible to me. It goes against the person I am. I am made for healing, not wounding someone else. So, something for me and you to consider is, why would we ever look to anyone who speaks cruelly to others as an accurate source of truth for who we are? Don't go to abusive people for input or insights about who you are. Anyone who would treat others the way narcissists and their flying monkeys do is clearly not a person who comes from a place of love, and therefore cannot be trusted. They will never be able to see you clearly, and that's okay. It is possible to be okay with that.

The more you allow them to live in their deluded dramas and pathological lies without attaching to their behavior, the more you will be free to create a life that reflects who you really are. They are choosing their path. Now you get to choose yours.

It is possible to be okay with someone else not seeing you clearly. It is possible to live a beautiful life even while others believe lies about you. Their behavior has nothing to do with you. Consider accepting everything in your life just the way it is right now. Change what you can change and allow the rest to just be. The narcissist and his or her flying monkeys will have to live with their own choices and the consequences that naturally come from them. You get to move on, knowing the truth about yourself and choosing to be with those who see it too.

CHAPTER SIXTEEN

Rewriting Destructive Messages

W E RECEIVE MANY DESTRUCTIVE MESSAGES from narcissists. If you were with a covert narcissist these messages were relayed to you in more subtle ways. You may not be aware of some of the messages you received about yourself. My hope is this chapter will help you recognize these negative messages, show you that they have nothing to do with who you are, and help you rewrite these messages.

I asked members of my online support group to share the destructive messages they received about themselves from the narcissists in their lives. Below, I list many of their responses because I have a feeling that what you have been told or was implied to you about yourself will be on this list. There are common messages narcissists give to targets and this list includes many of them.

It is helpful to hear what others have experienced. It helps validate what we have gone through and opens our eyes to how horrific and untrue these statements are. It also helps us recognize this is a narcissistic pattern and has nothing to do with us. We get used to believing what we are told by people we think know us and care about us, and we lose sight of who we really are.

After you read these messages, I will lead you through questions that will help you sort out the truth. Then I will share an exercise and recommendation that will help you rewrite these messages.

If you find yourself being triggered, or feeling strong and overwhelming emotions as you read the list, take a break. Be with yourself. Do some exercises for your nervous system such as those I described earlier. Speak to yourself and say things like, "I love you. Everything is going to be okay. I am loved. What I experienced was not love, and I am worthy of love." Repeat these if you need to until you feel your body settle down.

Here are the messages people in the group shared that they have received from narcissists:

Never good enough
I am too decadent.

I take too much care of myself.

I don't work hard enough.

I am too dramatic.

Too sensitive

Selfish

Materialistic

I wanted too much.

I am not worthy of love.

My needs and wants didn't matter.

He didn't want me to outshine him.

I was lazy.

I depended too much on him.

I was boring.

I was a nag to our kids.

I was too negative.

My feelings, let alone my pain, was all irrelevant.

I am rigid and controlling, making me a very difficult person.
"If you would just lighten up."

I was controlling.

He said I was addicted to passion, drama queen, too sensitive,
too into my feelings, too dramatic.

He would always say that I was uncoordinated, that I had horrible decorating tastes. That I wasn't creative at all, that I wasn't athletic.

I was not supportive enough of his career.

I got the message that I was a huge screw-up in every way.

I was too fat after having children.

The house was never clean enough.

I am too loud, too sensitive, too lazy, had the wrong interests, not organized enough, not exercising enough.

I was overthinking things, imagining stuff, creating scenarios in my head, and tormenting them and myself.

I was childish.

I was controlling, naggy, and someone who "kept" bringing things up.

I wanted too much (time/attention/affection/respect).

I was a pushover and lazy, not good enough, couldn't clean the house as well as others could.

I was a brat, dependent, confrontational, a child, stupid, loud, irrational, lazy, and recently during the divorce manipulative and a liar.

I was told I didn't live in the real world.

I was not good at working with people.

I was a problem.

He kept telling people I'm a whale and should lose weight.

My accomplishments were not worth celebrating.

I shouldn't talk in public.

I wasn't enough... not successful, stylish, funny, ambitious, attractive, wealthy, relaxed, or capable enough for him.

I only thought about myself.

I was childlike, immature.

I lived in a bubble with rose-colored glasses.

I wasn't sexual enough therefore I had no ability to provide him the intimacy he needed.

I had no empathy for him.

I was stubborn.

I was too happy.

I was too emotional.

I was too dramatic, too sensitive, took things too personally.

I was too much of a dreamer instead of a realist, I was seeking conflict, I needed to "better myself."

I was controlling and too sensitive/dramatic.

Always implied I never appreciated him

Subtle messages that when I was ill it was an overreaction or somehow my fault.

I was difficult or demanding when I set a boundary or expressed disagreement.

I was dumb, an airhead, forgetful.

My "sexual dysfunction" was a mental health issue that I needed to spend thousands of dollars on therapy to correct all while he sat around waiting for me to "fix myself."

That I'm lazy for needing mental health days off, for needing to sleep in after working on a project until 3am, for getting sick, for having injuries, for needing any rest ever.

You are broken. You are damaged goods.

You are a burden that I bear only because I love you SOOOO much.

Your dreams don't matter, your feelings don't matter, you are not enough, you should be doing more, you aren't doing a good job with our finances.

I am controlling. I am worthless. I am not loved. I am not enough.

From my mom: I was ugly, stupid, too emotional, moody, a slob, lazy, I had terrible taste in clothes, hair, makeup, not worthy of love or any attention at all.

I couldn't do anything right.

I was not sexy enough.

I am vain and lazy and manipulate with tears.

You are lazy. You should be able to take care of yourself when you are sick.

I was told I was jealous, controlling, and negative.

Too emotional. Fake. Messy and disorganized. Bad with money. Lots of mental health issues. Needy.

I needed a thicker skin.

I was too emotional.

I was the crazy one.

I am unlovable and should be so grateful anyone can stand to be around me.

Lazy, disorganized, materialistic, terrible with budgeting

I have a bad body.

I don't know how to dress.

I'm bad at being feminine.

I'm crazy.

I'm jealous.

I'm ignorant.

I am too sensitive.

I was impossible to please.

I was too open, no filter, embarrassing.

I was someone to be ashamed of.

I'm crazy, I'm overly emotional, reactive, and sensitive.

I wasn't a trophy wife, that I was fat.

I was pathetic.

I'm too controlling.

I don't know how to love.

I can't take a joke.

I was selfish, controlling, angry, withholding, envious, status oriented, mistrusting, insatiable.

I am too sensitive. Too angry. Too mean.

I have too much energy.

I need too much taking care of.

I needed help.

I was/am unattractive.

I am not as good as I think I am.

Not good enough

I was lazy, selfish, and too sensitive.

Too sensitive, codependent, controlling

I was lazy, boring, and dishonest.

Too sensitive, too needy, controlling and manipulative, too slow to forgive, overreacting to everything.......and the list goes on

Incapable, lazy, cold, stupid.

I was too emotional and can't think clearly.

I am sexually undesirable.

I should be grateful that I was with him because who else would want me.

I am too needy and require too much reassurance.

I am only nice to people because I want them to owe me favors in the future or for them to be indebted to me.

I am too open and honest. I should keep my mouth shut.

I don't know anything about finances.

I am dramatic, hard to love, hard to please.

I am too sensitive, too kind, too soft, too caring, not fit enough, not fashionable enough, rubbish at telling a story, take too long to get to my point always, too risk averse, lazy, not good enough, idealist.

I am weak and wishy washy.

"Hasn't mummy got a big nose." "Where's mummy, in bed again?"

I am too sensitive, the meanest person he ever met, too lazy, too controlling, always overreacting, always say the wrong thing in front of other people.

I was too narcissistic, too selfish.

I was overly dramatic.

Not good enough

I always had to have things my way.

I am toxic.

I was never happy enough.

I was unattractive, unimportant, inadequate, incompetent, selfish, domineering.

I was stupid.

I was not loving enough.

Too dramatic

Not very attractive to him

Not sexy

Not calm or controlled enough

Too emotional

Too loud

Too distracted

Too sensitive

Too aggressive

Too passive

Too much

I didn't matter.

Never. Good. Enough.

Nothing I wanted for myself mattered.

Too sensitive and overweight

Hypersensitive, selfish, uncaring, and controlling

"I work, you do nothing..."

I don't do anything. I have trust issues. I'm a control freak.

I don't matter.

I am unlikable, unworthy of love.

I am not worth the effort.

*I was not worthy of love, a burden to everyone including my
    parents and sisters, useless, worthless, dumb.*

I was lazy and shirking my chores.

Over dramatic

My sexuality is shameful.

*Too needy, too sensitive, too complicated, too demanding,
    too naggy, too much work.*

Ungrateful, not a thoughtful daughter.

I have too much and don't deserve it.

I am insignificant and not worth listening to.

I was too picky.

Too needy

Controlling, selfish, not being empathetic to her needs

I don't matter.

Undesirable

Not good enough

Worthless

I am disposable.

I was not lovable.

I was a burden. My needs were inconvenient. My wants were stupid.

I was too much, too loud, too confident, too caring, too generous.

I was a worthless piece of sh*t.

I was crazy.

I don't make enough money.

In the divorce decree, he said I abandoned the marriage.

I am ugly, worthless, stupid, incompetent, a shameful burden.

My happiness is not important.

I was damaged goods.

Never enough

I'm fat.

I'm unhealthy.

I'm unmotivated to get a career.

I'm a messily gross person.

I don't listen.

I don't obey.

I'm dramatic.

I'm crazy.

I am controlling.

I am possessive.

I am needy.

I am in bad shape.

I'm hella lazy.

I am not worthy of basic healthy communication.

I am a child.

I am an abuser.

Here are some exercises that will help you see that these messages have nothing to do with you:

1. Write down the negative messages you saw on the list that you received about yourself. Add any that were not on the list.

_____

_____

_____

_____

_____

_____

_____

_____

_____

_____

_____

_____

_____

_____

2. From the messages you listed in #1, write down which are true of the narcissist in your life.

3. From your list in #1, write the messages that attempt to keep you down and keep you from shining, feeling good, and being happy.

4. Now it's time to rewrite these messages. Take all the messages you received that you recorded in #1 and write the opposite of those statements below. For instance, if you were told you were lazy, write *I am not lazy.* If you'd like you can add truths next to this like, *I am a hard worker. I am dedicated. I am productive.* To take this further, feel free to add evidence for your brain to see that this is true. For example, *I work hard to keep this home clean, I do so much for my kids, I worked hard on* _____.
I put a lot of effort and time into my relationships. Whatever is true for you. It is helpful for our brain to see examples that make the statement, "I am not lazy" true.

For messages such as You are too sensitive, you can write something like, *I am sensitive, and I love that about myself. Sensitive people are a gift to the world. I am a gift to the world.* Write whatever is true of you, in your own words.

Let's say you have been put down for your size. Maybe you weigh more than you would like. You can write something like, *I weigh more than I would like to right now, and that is okay. It is not a reflection of my value or my worth, or whether I deserve to be loved. I deserve to be loved at any size. I am perfect just the way I am. No one has the right to tell me what size I need to be.*

Use this space to turn around the destructive messages you have received in whatever way feels good to you. Use words that feel like love—words that are kind and compassionate toward yourself.

Chapter Sixteen: Rewriting Destructive Messages

_____

_____

_____

_____

_____

_____

_____

_____

_____

_____

_____

_____

_____

_____

_____

_____

_____

_____

_____

_____

_____

_____

_____

_____

_____

_____

_____

_____

When you feel complete with your positive statements, I recommend writing them on a piece of paper and keep this list by your bed. Every morning as you wake up, reach for this paper of truth and read it to yourself. Let the healing words soak in. The more you do this, the more your brain and body will accept these statements as truth. To help with this, I have created a guided meditation that helps rewrite many of the false messages we receive from narcissists. This meditation can be found on my website and is mentioned on the resource page at the end of this book.

Remember, all the negative things you heard about yourself have nothing to do with you. These messages are reflections of the unhappiness inside the narcissist. You don't need to take any of these on. You are not what you have been told.

The truth is you are stunning. You are a beautiful soul. You are a gift, and the world is lucky to have you.

CHAPTER SEVENTEEN

Learning to Trust Yourself

TRUSTING OURSELVES is the most challenging and important skill we can learn. I cannot overstate how important and crucial this is. People often ask me, "How can I guard and protect myself from getting involved with another narcissist?" My number one answer is to master the art of trusting yourself.

You can learn all the traits, the red flags, have all the information in your mind, but if you don't trust yourself, you can still fall prey to covert manipulation.

I also don't want to understate the amount of strength and courage it takes to trust yourself, especially when other people don't see the truth, and on the outside everything looks fine. This applies even beyond our personal relationships to a larger scale. So many people are unaware of all the covert manipulation that is taking place in our world today.

I am beginning to realize the gift we have been given with this relatively new knowledge of covert narcissism. We need this information more than ever because we will be able to see through things that most of humanity won't. We, as people who have experienced narcissistic abuse, are more awake and alert to red flags than others who have not been through this. Our wisdom and strength are needed more than ever.

Many of us are empathic. Our bodies feel when things are off. I believe all of us have that innate ability. We have just learned to distrust it and override it with our intellect and conditioning.

Being with a narcissist, or being raised by one, teaches you to not trust yourself. There is so much cognitive dissonance, it becomes difficult to see and know what is true. In addition to that, being gaslighted furthers our mistrust in our ability to believe ourselves.

So, how can we change this and learn to trust our gut, our bodily reactions, and our own innate intelligence? It takes practice and a new mindset.

First, you need to know that your body is incredibly intelligent. There have been numerous scientific studies that show this. Our bodies know the truth before our conscious mind does. That is why many reach a point over time, if they were in a romantic relationship with a narcissist, where they no longer have a desire to have sex with them. If you experienced this, you probably thought something was wrong with you, and I'm sure they encouraged that destructive and false belief. The truth is there is nothing wrong with you, and in fact, so much is right with you. Your body knew you were not emotionally safe with them, so it shut down. It was trying to protect you.

When you look back, there were probably many times when you felt things were off, but your mind talked you out of it. That is completely understandable, so please give yourself grace around this. Narcissists are master manipulators and can fool the smartest, most intuitive people.

Learning to trust yourself takes conscious effort and time. It's like strengthening a new muscle. It begins with slowly and gently adding the new habit of becoming aware of your body. Most of us go through our days feeling detached from our body. We are not consciously aware of the amazing vehicle we inhabit, and as a result often do not notice the body's signals, the messages it is trying to alert us to.

One way you can become more aware in your body is to take brief moments throughout your day to stop and notice you have legs, look at your hands, notice parts of your body. When you are doing simple things like walking, or picking something up with your hands, observe how your body moves so effortlessly, and your subconscious mind knows what to do.

Begin to notice sensations in your body when you are around other people. Become aware of how different parts of your body feel when you recall a memory. How do they change when the memory is happy or sad? How do you feel in different places? How does your body feel in nature compared to a store or an office building? I find this interesting to do when I travel, noticing how I feel in different cities, states, and countries.

This will also help your nervous system. You can combine these moments with the times you hold your hand and say, "This is my hand, this is my body."

The more you notice and connect with your body the more in tune with it you will become. Then when you are with someone and they say something that sounds normal, but your body has a reaction—like your stomach tightens or your head feels unclear, or your shoulders feel weak—you will notice, because you've become so aware of your body. This will also build trust in the relationship you have with yourself, which will in turn bring a feeling of safety, which will help regulate your nervous system. It all works together so beautifully.

Another thing you can do to learn to trust your body is take time to ask yourself, "What are you feeling right now?" If you don't know the answer, that's okay. Just you asking the question will begin to build awareness and connect you to your emotions, which will create a relationship with yourself where you will be able to live in harmony with all your feelings.

These new habits and ways of being with yourself will change your life in so many profound ways, and will protect you from unhealthy and destructive people.

Another great question to ask your body during the day is, "What do you need right now?" Be curious. You don't have to have an answer; just like the previous question, the act of asking lets your body, your heart, know that you care. It builds trust and makes you aware of your needs. This is another form of self-care. If you do hear or feel a response, honor your body's needs and desires.

Learning to trust yourself is a journey, but it is worth the time and effort. You are worth the time and effort.

CHAPTER EIGHTEEN

Boundaries

LEARNING AND INCORPORATING HEALTHY BOUNDARIES is so important to the healing process. You are relearning who you are and awakening to what you have really been through. Setting up clear guidelines for your new life will give you space and safety to effectively move forward.

When we set boundaries for ourselves, we are showing the parts of us that feel afraid that they are safe, that we are in charge, and that we will be our protector. When we feel taken care of and looked after in this way, our body relaxes.

When you are healing, it is crucial to have boundaries when it comes to the people you allow into your life. You are the author and director of your life, and you get to choose who is allowed to be a part of it. You have the right to say who you want by your side and who you don't.

As trauma expert Peter A. Levine writes in his book, *Healing Trauma*, "When we are traumatized, we need support, not judgement."

You have been through a tremendous amount, and more than ever you need people around you who are supportive, loving, kind, and respectful.

You don't need to explain yourself or defend yourself to anyone anymore. It is too exhausting, and people who truly know you and love you will never put you in a position where you have to defend who you are.

If someone asks you to do something you are not comfortable doing, you have the right to say no, and you don't owe them a reason. You have the power to choose to do things you want to do and not do things that don't feel good or right to you.

It is important to get clear on what behavior is acceptable to you, and what is not okay with you.

Here are some examples of behaviors that are never okay and should never be allowed. There is no reason for anyone to yell at you or physically harm you. Anyone who belittles you, demeans you, or puts you down in any way is no longer allowed. You have the right to tell anyone to leave your home and your life at any time, and you don't owe toxic people an explanation.

I invite you to welcome into your life people who really see you, value you, cherish you, respect you, and always—and I mean always—treat you with kindness.

Here are some questions to help you get clear on your boundaries:

1. What qualities are your "must-haves" for people close to you?

_____

_____

_____

_____

_____

_____

_____

_____

_____

_____

_____

2. What will you not tolerate or allow in your life from now on?

_____

_____

_____

_____

_____

_____

_____

_____

_____

_____

_____

_____

_____

_____

This also goes for the way you speak to and treat yourself. Part of learning boundaries is having guidelines for yourself as to what you will and won't allow. For example, I have become vigilant about not allowing any unkind words out of my own mouth, or in my thoughts toward myself. I no longer permit belittling, demeaning, or disrespectful words. If I find myself thinking anything negative about or toward myself, I will stop and say, "I'm sorry. Forgive me. I love you. Thank you." I end by saying "Thank you" to show gratitude toward myself for bringing this to my attention so I can turn things around and fill myself with loving statements. This idea comes from an ancient Hawaiian healing method called Hooponopono.

Sometimes I say these words repeatedly until my body feels safe, loved, and taken care of.

3. What are some ways you put yourself down?

_____

_____

_____

_____

_____

_____

_____

_____

_____

_____

_____

_____

4. What are some new loving messages you can give yourself?

_____

_____

_____

_____

_____

_____

_____

_____

_____

Along with setting boundaries with who you let in your life and how you treat yourself, it is important to set boundaries with the narcissist from whom you are walking away.

If you have children with them, make sure to set clear lines. They will use your connection as a parent and your children to wound you, to get you riled up, to tear you down, and to drain your energy. Be clear about behavior from them that you will not tolerate. It may be a good idea to talk this over with an attorney. Tell them what you think would be best for the children and see what options you have to ensure the best plan for their mental health as well as yours.

One boundary that is important is to never talk about emotions or personal things with the narcissist. Keep it to business. Keep it brief. They may try to start arguments with you. Don't fall for it. Become boring and non-emotional around them—this technique is referred to as the grey rock method. When you engage with them, talk to them in a way that is uninteresting. This way you won't give them any of your energy.

If you don't have children together, or your kids are older, the best and most loving boundary for yourself is to have no contact with the narcissist. Leaving a person with NPD is like leaving a cult. You still have a lot of programming and brainwashing to unravel. The longer you don't see them or hear their voice, the more you will be able to see through the lies, the manipulation, and control. If you see them, it's like going back to the cult compound. All the confusion and old tapes will come rushing back. You need complete time away so you can have a chance to be with yourself and think for yourself.

Boundaries are about showing respect for yourself by guarding your energy. It is also important to notice the things and people in your life that drain you, along with who and what bring you energy. Below are questions that will help you explore what areas in your life may need some boundaries.

Taking Inventory of Your Life

1. List the people in your life who drain your energy:

_____

_____

_____

_____

_____

_____

_____

_____

_____

2. List the people in your life who lift you up—those who leave you with more energy after being with them or talking with them:

_____

_____

_____

_____

_____

_____

_____

3. List activities that drain your energy:

4. List activities that energize you or bring you peace and calm:

When I think of boundaries, I picture myself standing guard at the door of my life. I am protecting my heart, my dreams, my longings, and my life-force energy. I am committed to being there for myself. May you begin to see yourself as the guardian of your precious heart—a fierce protector, always standing up for you, always being there for you as an ever-present loyal friend.

CHAPTER NINETEEN

Relearning What Love Looks Like through Self-Care and Self-Love

IMMERSING YOUR BODY AND HEART IN SELF-LOVE and self-care is essential for healing after narcissistic abuse. You have been treated so badly for so long, it is time to turn that around for yourself and relearn what real love looks and feels like.

This will do a few things. It will help safeguard you against getting involved with narcissists or other toxic and draining people in the future because you will get so used to how good love feels, you won't want to settle for anything less than what you are giving to yourself.

It will also help your body heal physically and emotionally. Our bodies are designed for love. We thrive when we feel good. Our immune system weakens when we feel bad, to put it simply. This is evidence that shows we are meant to feel good.

The third thing immersing yourself in self-love and self-care will do for you is help rewrite a common story we get from narcissists. Most of us come away from these people believing we don't deserve to be happy, that we aren't worthy of being treated well. This is a lie, and loving yourself and giving yourself nurturing care will help you see that you are worthy of feeling wonderful, of enjoying your life, and of being loved.

Become vigilant about how you speak to yourself. Use words of kindness, compassion, and understanding.

Treat yourself to experiences that bring you joy and comfort, such as walks by the ocean, hiking through forests or mountains, or sitting by a stream. Drinking your favorite tea. Curling up with a book you get lost in. Indulging in long baths. Candlelit evenings. Your favorite music. Massaging yourself with luxurious oils. Soaking your feet in water. Taking time to look at the stars at night. Sitting by a campfire. Meeting up with a good friend. Anything that brings a smile to your face. Anything that feels calming and nurturing.

If you are someone who has been taught that self-care is selfish, let me assure you that loving yourself and taking care of your body and heart is the most helpful thing you can do not only for yourself, but for others as well. When you take care of yourself and fill yourself with love, you will naturally become more loving to others. You will have more patience, more energy, and more wisdom and kindness to share. You will also be an inspiration for others, especially for your children. Modeling this behavior will help them see that they are also worthy of taking care of themselves.

Self-love and self-care are not the same as being selfish. When you are a naturally giving person, taking care of yourself and loving yourself will only give you more energy to help others. It will also provide you with wisdom as to how you can help in a way that does not drain your energy and affect your health in a negative way.

Relearning a healthy balance of giving and receiving what your body and heart needs is so important after narcissistic abuse. The more you give yourself love and care, the more you will be able to see and feel that healthy balance. This is all part of relearning what love really looks like.

You deserve to know the true picture of love. Your body deserves to feel it. It was made for it. Your mind deserves to know the difference. And your heart. Your beautiful, important heart needs to be held like never before.

CHAPTER TWENTY

The In-Between

ONCE WE DISCOVER that we have been dealing with a narcissist in our life and become more educated on the traits, as well as more loving with ourselves, we begin to notice other people in our life who also have narcissistic traits. Some we have known for a long time but have not realized this about them until now. With our more educated eyes we start to reevaluate who we spend time with, and ultimately begin letting go of some relationships.

One day I was on the phone with a friend I have known for a long time. It had been a while since we had spoken. She talked about a memory we shared years ago. I told her I didn't remember that. She laughed hysterically for what felt like a bizarrely long time. She kept saying she couldn't believe I didn't remember. It was a mocking, devaluing laugh. Instead of reacting, I stayed in my body and noticed how bad this felt to me. I had become so used to the feeling of love and unconditional acceptance of myself. I had also become used to being present in my body. In the past I would have defended myself or laughed awkwardly with her and wondered if something was wrong with my brain. This time I stayed quiet and observed. I let her laugh and decided to say nothing and just watch to see where she took the conversation. It occurred to me that she might be gaslighting me. I flashed to other conversations we had over the years where she brought up my memory and mocked it. The thing is, there is no one else in my life who ever brings up my memory to me as an issue. Only her. I ended the call soon after that and sat with myself.

I decided to pull back from this relationship and use the grey rock method during any further contact.

Over the years my eyes have opened to other relationships in my life, and I have ended some. Others I have decided to keep but have limited interaction with. I have noticed I have a pattern in me where I tend to give more than I receive in relationships. My standards have raised for all my relationships as my respect for myself has grown.

This is common for many of us survivors, and it leaves us in an often-unsettling in-between place. This time in our lives of raising our standards and clearing people out of our lives can feel lonely. But it is an important step toward creating a life that honors our heart.

This is a gap period between our old life and a new, more heart-honoring way of living. As we grow, our old relationships will be affected. Narcissists will be exposed because they don't like to have friends who are strong and self-confident.

The more love we show ourselves, the more we will be able to see through the behavior of others, and the more we will crave healthy and loving friendships and romantic partners.

If you are in this in-between time, be very proud of yourself. It takes courage to let go of people and stand on our own. The good news is, by doing this you are making room for new friendships, new loves to come into your life. And while you are waiting, or pausing, you can use this special time to be with yourself in a very tender way. You can use this sacred space to explore what it is you really want in new relationships, in all areas of your life. You can reassure yourself that this time is temporary. You are pruning your garden of all that inhibits beauty and life from thriving.

You deserve to have people in your life who love you, treat you with respect, and feel lucky to have you in their life. Be patient. Be choosy. They will come.

CHAPTER TWENTY-ONE

The Perks of Being on Your Own

I t CAN BE SCARY TO LEAVE A NARCISSIST. For some people it is a clear decision to leave and they never look back. Others feel conflicted and fearful about leaving. They wonder if they aren't seeing the narcissist accurately, and if they are actually letting go of a truly wonderful person. This is more common if the narcissist is covert. Some wonder if they didn't try hard enough. If you feel any of these things, it is likely due to the narcissist manipulating you to see things in these ways, along with the cognitive dissonance you are most likely experiencing.

If the narcissist's tactics were subtler, it can generate even more fear. *Am I making the right decision? Am I over-dramatizing things? Is the problem really with me? How am I going to support myself? Will I be alone the rest of my life?*

No matter what type of relationship you had with someone with NPD, whether they were a parent, sibling, friend, coworker, or lover, the result is the same—complete disempowerment, and as a result, often crippling fear.

One thing to remind yourself of is the fact that fear never comes from love. Any confusion you may have, any doubts that still exist can be laid to rest when you realize that if you were truly loved by this person, if they really were a "great catch," you would not be feeling the turmoil you feel right now.

You deserve to be with someone who treats you well. Life is too short to spend it with someone who despises you and leaves you feeling the way you are right now.

If you are feeling fearful about leaving a narcissist and being on your own, I want to help shift your perspective and open your eyes and heart to the perks that come from leaving. It is completely understandable to feel fear, and it is helpful to look at the great things that will come from leaving them. Here are several considerations to get you started thinking in a positive direction. At the end of the list, feel free to add any more perks that come to mind.

1. You now have a chance to get your energy back.

When you live with a narcissist, no matter how much work you do on yourself to heal, you can still feel their toxic and draining energy. It is difficult to stay afloat in the midst of their demeaning and devaluing behavior. Just being in the same space with them depletes you of your life-force energy, especially if you are a sensitive or empathic person. It is like you're swimming in the ocean and every time you make it to the surface of the water, a wave comes and pushes you back down. When you are on your own, you have a chance to breathe, collect your thoughts, rest, and be with yourself. You have time and space to be able to pay attention to what you need.

2. You have the freedom to make your own decisions.

You get to choose how you decorate your home. You get to choose what you do with your time. You get to choose how you spend, save, and invest your money. You get to choose how you dress, who you spend your time with, and where you want to live. You get to have a messy room or a clean room. You can paint your walls pink, or green, or whatever color thrills you. It is all your choice now. You are free. Free from judgment, free from condescending looks, free from devaluing and demeaning comments, free from the silent treatment, gaslighting, and walking on eggshells. You can exhale now knowing you oversee your life, and you get to choose everything.

3. You get to choose how your home feels.

You no longer have to feel that oppressive energy lying next to you, or as you walk into your home. You can now fill your home with candles, your favorite teas, incense with an aroma that delights your senses. You can play calming music. You can surround yourself with life-giving plants. You get to decide how your home feels without any interference. If you have children, you get to choose the energy of the home you all live in. What a gift that is to them and you. They will always remember how your home felt, and how they felt in it with you.

4. You now have a chance to heal.

You can now take time for yourself. You have removed the drama from your life, the noise. Now you can be with yourself and become your own caretaker, your own refuge. You now have space and time to cry, to grieve, to be your full self. You have room to let out all the feelings that come up for you. Now you can treat those feelings with compassion and empathy. You can take time to rewrite the untrue messages you've received about yourself and about life. You can let down and exhale. You can do what your heart needs and longs for.

5. You get to discover new dreams.

If you were married to a narcissist, you may have believed this was your forever person. Divorce was something you would have never imagined. You were dedicated, you gave your whole heart to them and to the relationship, firmly believing this would never end. You loved them with every fiber of your being. Your future always included them. Now it might feel like your future is empty and those dreams are gone. Here is a different way of looking at it. You get to dream again. A fresh, new dream. And this time it doesn't include someone who doesn't love you. As you heal and feel your body settling down, you can take time to reassess your vision for your future. You are letting go of a life you thought you had, but in fact was an illusion.

And now you get to build something that is the real thing. This will be a new adventure of getting to know what you long for now. You are a different person at this point in your life, and you have a chance to discover what lights you up and energizes your heart. So, dream away, my dear friend, for you deserve a new vision, a new reality that lines up perfectly with who you are now.

6.   You now have a chance to experience real love.

You have had the antithesis of love, and now you get to feel the real thing. This journey begins with you. You can relearn love, create a new template for love. This begins with kindness toward yourself, compassion, and unconditional acceptance of exactly who you are in this moment. Be fiercely loyal to yourself. Pamper your body. Hold yourself. Free yourself from all judgment, shame, and doubt. You are perfect just the way you are. There is nothing that needs to be added to you or taken away for you to be valuable and worthy of love. Your journey is to discover the magnificence that lies within you. And when you are ready to date again, it will be different this time. You had the courage and strength to leave, and because you did, you've given yourself another chance to be truly loved by someone who is head over heels in love with you.

7.   You get to see how strong you are.

You might be feeling weak and afraid right now, and I so understand that. I've been there. This type of abuse pushes you to your lowest lows, often at just the time when you need your strength most. I have found targets of narcissists to be some of the strongest people I've ever met. You have been made to feel weak for too long, but you will see your innate strength rise just when you need it most. You will find people coming into your life at just the right time. Resources will show up when you need them. Through this process of awakening to what you have been through and learning to value yourself, to stand up for yourself, you will find a strength in you that you did not know you had. And one day you will turn around, look at all you've been through, and marvel. You will energetically bow to yourself, and say, *Wow. You are amazing. I am so proud and impressed with you!*

Leaving a narcissist takes an incredible amount of strength and you may not feel it right now, but trust me, you have it in spades. You will make it through this, and you will see how incredibly strong you are.

Use this space to add any additional perks that come to mind:

CHAPTER TWENTY-TWO

Relearning Who You Are

RECENTLY SPOKE WITH A WOMAN IN HER SEVENTIES who had just finalized her divorce after being in a marriage with a narcissist for most of her adult life. "I don't even know who I am anymore. I don't even know what I like. I feel completely lost," she said with a despairing tone.

After being with a narcissist it is common to feel this way. We have spent so much of our time putting our attention and energy on them and getting swirled up in their unnecessary dramas. We have also been given a false picture of who we really are. We are traumatized and as a result have a difficult time seeing clearly.

If you feel lost and confused as to who are you, please know this is not your fault. There is nothing wrong with you. How you feel is completely normal and natural after all you've been through. Give yourself grace and time to rediscover who you are.

Part of the healing process includes a tender time of rediscovery. We need to relearn what lights us up, what we are interested in, what brings us joy, and what gives us energy.

You have heard and felt a lot of lies about who you are and now it is time to be with yourself and learn the truth about important you.

There is only one you. Become curious about yourself. Come to yourself with complete acceptance and be intrigued with what you will discover. You have a fresh start.

One practical exercise to help you get reacquainted with yourself is to create an energy jar. You could also use a basket, bowl, vase, or whatever container makes you smile. At the end of each day, write down on a small piece of paper something you noticed that day that brought you to life. Fold it up and place it in the container of your choice. Keep adding more each day and you will build a collection of all the things that bring you energy. Periodically you can read through the treasures you have discovered about yourself.

Noticing and learning these things will begin to change the way you live your life, often without trying. It will happen naturally. The more you see the things and people that affect you in a positive way, the more you will want them in your life.

Here are some questions for you to answer that will help you begin to explore more about who you are.

1. What places have you visited where you noticed yourself feeling more energy and smiling?

_____

_____

_____

_____

_____

_____

_____

_____

_____

_____

_____

_____

_____

_____

2. What activities help you feel calm, relaxed, and peaceful?

3. Who in your life do you feel loves and accepts you
   unconditionally?

4. When was the last time you felt good? What was happening at that time to cause you to feel that way?

5. Whose life looks like one you would like to have? What elements of their life sound and look wonderful to you?

6. What do you daydream about? Do you notice any common themes?

7. What were some of the happiest times in your life? What about these moments contributed to you feeling really good?

CHAPTER TWENTY-THREE

Where I Am Now with My Healing

WHEN YOU ARE IN THE MIDST OF THE DEEPEST PAIN, it is difficult to see the light at the end of the tunnel, so I want to explain what changes I see in myself now compared to several years ago when I went through the discard. I am hoping that as you hear about where I am today, you will feel hope and encouragement to keep going. You will see that you won't always feel the way you do right now. You will know that profound healing and freedom are possible.

I am a different person today than I was when I first discovered covert narcissism and began to unravel what I had been through. I feel calmer inside. Things have settled down in my body and mind. I see more clearly now what I experienced in the different relationships I have had throughout my life with covert narcissists. I am stronger. I am more in tune with my heart and body. I trust myself more than ever. I am very selective as to who I allow in my life now, who I open my heart to, and who I choose to be intimate with. I feel more open to life, more trusting of it. I feel more trusting of myself to be able to navigate it.

I now have a love for myself that brings tears to my eyes. I treat myself with compassion, understanding, and unconditional love. I know now that nothing is wrong with me. I am lovable and worthy of kindness, respect, and love, and I feel that more than ever.

I believe everything I have experienced with these types of people was for a reason, and I am grateful now for all the lessons I have learned and am continuing to learn. All I have been through, and where I have taken my pain, confusion, and sadness has become the making of me. I am proud of myself for doing the healing work. I am proud of myself for remaining a kind, gentle, open-hearted, and good person. I am proud of myself for having the strength and courage to walk away from abuse. I have been through an incredible amount, in my intimate relationships and throughout my childhood, and I make sure to honor my heart by acknowledging all I have been through.

I honor all my emotions. Even though I experience more peace in my life now, fears, worries, and anxious thoughts still show up. The difference is that now I know how to be with my emotions. I take time when thoughts come up that bring me anxiety. I hold my hand and say, "This is my hand. This is my body." I tune in and ask what my heart needs. I don't judge myself for my thoughts and feelings. I come to all my emotions with unconditional acceptance, love, understanding, and compassion. I know there is an understandable reason I am feeling what I am, and I know my heart deserves attention, time, and care.

I know now that the messages I received from narcissists about my emotions are untrue. I understand they came from people who are uncomfortable with their own emotions and projected their issues onto me. It had nothing to do with me. I see myself as the caretaker of my body, and part of my job is to continue to be a safe place for whatever feelings show up in me.

Memories of abuse still come to my mind from time to time, but how I feel when they show up is different. For years I had painful flashbacks from past relationships that would feel like trauma reentering my body. They would take me out. I felt like I was reliving the abuse all over again. Now, occasionally flashbacks will come, but my body doesn't react in the same way. It doesn't feel traumatized like it used to. It feels calm. It feels like the memories come to mind when I am ready to heal them. Now I know how to be with myself in a tender, strong, and caring way when such memories arise.

Another area of my life where I have seen change relates to my creativity. When you are with a narcissist, your creativity is suppressed. You are in survival mode so much of the time, your creative self has no room or space to shine through. Since I left the toxic relationship I was in, my ability to create has been like nothing I've seen before. This often happens in stage three, the Dreaming and Rebuilding Phase that I am in now.

When I look back it was like my life was in black and white and now there is so much color. I have become a thunderstorm of creation. I felt caged for so long, and now it's like I've been set free and I can explore and access all these creative ideas in me. When we are constantly demeaned and devalued it is difficult to see the well of jewels we all have within us. There is so much that is just waiting to come out.

In addition to dampening your creativity, another effect of being with a narcissist is that your desires are belittled and not respected. Your desires, especially your deep, afraid-to-say-out-loud desires, cravings, and longings are incredibly important. They are the keys to unlock your fullest potential so you can experience life at its very best. Your desires are part of an important picture that make you who you are. I believe we are all here for a reason and I also believe that our desires, the things we are drawn to, things we dream about, things that light us up are the breadcrumbs, the clues we have that reveal and lead us to why we are here.

We are taught by narcissists to give our energy to them and that to give it to ourselves is selfish and egotistical. We learn to equate going after things we love as being self-focused, when in fact, if we all did the things that brought us life and joy, the frequency of this planet would reach such a joyous level and living here would take on a harmonious and magical feeling.

I now pay attention to what brings me life, what makes my heart sing, and see the value for myself in me pursuing my dreams. I don't see this as selfish anymore. I see now that the more alive I feel, the more this helps me and others.

We have been held down by others for far too long. Our desires and dreams are worthy of our attention. The more we move toward the things that make us smile, the more we help lift our own energy and that of this planet and all those around us. The ripple effect is profound.

As we pursue our heart's desires, it is so important to work with people who support and encourage our vision, those who provide a space where we feel free to create. We deserve to be with people who believe in us.

Another area where I have changed a lot is with setting healthy boundaries. This is a work in progress for me, as is learning to not give my power away to other people. I am now aware that I have the propensity to give my power away to others, letting them have authority over me. Learning to be my own authority and trusting myself fully is an ongoing lesson for me. I catch myself faster now when I notice myself doing this. As with anything, I feel no judgment, only compassion and understanding. I have been set up in so many ways to give my power away, so I know this will take time to really master, and I am extending a huge amount of grace to myself because of that.

I am also learning that it is okay for me to disappoint people. In fact, it is necessary for my health that I learn this. According to Dr. Gabor Maté, in the documentary *The Wisdom of Trauma*, "People who get cancer tend to be nice people who are more concerned with the emotional needs of others than their own. They have a hard time expressing anger and also they have this belief that they must not disappoint anybody." It is a big lesson for me to learn to not put others' emotional needs before my own. It is like they say on airplanes, place the oxygen mask on yourself first before you help someone else.

I have also learned I can get easily excited about a new friend or a new love, and it is important for me to take my time with new people. To really get to know them. To be alert for any red flags. I am learning to pay attention to how I feel around them. To monitor my energy and notice how it is affected by them.

I have learned through all this that I am not here to pour myself out to others to the point where it affects my health. I now know this is disrespectful to myself. I would never want that for people I love, so I need to give myself that same love and respect.

I absolutely love to help people, support people, give to people, but I am now more discerning as to who gets access to my time, my heart, and my resources.

I have become more vigilant about who I spend my time with as well, who is allowed in my life. I am more aware now of how different people affect me. I have let go of some, decreased time with others, and put my energy and time into people from whom I feel consistent love. They are the greatest gifts I could ever have, and I cherish them beyond words.

I now have boundaries around things I will not tolerate from people anymore. I have been running an online support group for a couple years now. Here and there issues come up, and each time, I add another guideline to the group in response to the new issue. My admin and I used to be more lenient, giving people the benefit of the doubt, but over time we have seen that we need clear lines and we need to reserve the right to remove people immediately if they go against the guidelines. The guidelines are clear and there to protect the members of the group, to keep the space as emotionally safe as possible. Members often tell us this is the safest online group they've ever experienced and that the guidelines give them freedom to be honest and vulnerable. This experience has taught me a lot in my own life. I have learned I need to have my own clear guidelines, or boundaries, and I reserve the right to remove anyone in my life who does not follow them.

Here are some behaviors that are never allowed in my life. No one is allowed to hit me or physically abuse me. Yelling at me is never okay. Someone who consistently drains me of my energy is not allowed in. Demeaning words and behavior will not be tolerated. Someone who thinks I need to change for us to be friends or lovers can exit my life immediately. Someone who talks negatively about me to others is removed. Anyone who judges how I live my life and tells me their way is the right way and I am doing it wrong is not permitted. Word salad speeches, gaslighting, manipulation, controlling, devaluing, and unkindness are no longer allowed in my life.

Here is what I do invite into my life now. People who are consistently kind to me, who treat me with respect. People who build me up. People with whom I feel safe to be my full self. People I can trust. Those who want the best for me. Those whose words are consistent with their actions. People who are easy to communicate with and are emotionally mature. People who genuinely enjoy me and want me in their lives. People who love me exactly the way I am right now.

The guidelines for my own life keep evolving, just like the support group. When a new life lesson comes my way, I add another guideline for myself. This way, like the members, I feel valued, safe, protected, and cared for. This results in me trusting myself more as well.

It is clear to me now that none of the negative messages I received about myself were true. They were projections of others' unresolved issues. They had nothing to do with me.

Now the only messages I trust about myself from others are the ones that come from love, for that is the most accurate measure of truth. If someone is not coming from a place of love, what they say and how they act is affected by that, so they cannot see the truth about you and me.

For so long I thought I was the reason relationships with narcissists didn't work. I believed the lies and the gaslighting. Now I see that I was an incredible gift to the people I was with. When I love someone, I love them with every fiber of my being. I am a lover, a giver, a caretaker, and a nurturer. I am someone who cares tremendously about the hearts of those I love. I provide a safe space for them to share their dreams, fears, and insecurities. When I hear their dreams, I want to move mountains to help make them come true, and when I hear their fears, everything in me springs into action to help them know they are safe and everything is going to be okay.

The narcissists I have experienced did not recognize the gifts they had in me, and I am okay with that now because I am able to recognize that this had nothing to do with me. Someone else's behavior and view of me has nothing to do with the actual truth of who I am.

I no longer see myself as someone who has so many things wrong with me, someone who needs to change for another to be able to love me and want to be with me. I know I am lovable and worthy of love just the way I am.

My perspective on the narcissists I have experienced has changed as well. I notice the more peace and compassionate self-love I experience, the more I find myself feeling sadness for them. It is clear to me now that things are not well with them, with their internal state. No matter how people appear or represent themselves, the way they treat others tells a lot about what is going on inside of them.

The truth is we all have free will. Some will choose the path of love and life, and some will choose a path of decay. We can only make those choices for ourselves.

People often ask me how long it takes to heal after this type of abuse. There is no one timeline for everyone. There are so many factors that go into how long it takes us to heal. It will take time. This is not an overnight healing. You have been through a lot. You have subconsciously developed beliefs that will need to be unraveled. Your physical body has been affected and will need attention and care. Your tender heart and nervous system need time to learn how to feel safe again.

The good news is your body is designed to heal. The more you spend time being gentle with yourself and applying what you have learned in this book, things will feel better and better.

The path to healing is a restorative one and you will feel and see changes in yourself along the way. Each step, each victory will feel wonderful. The pain will diminish, and the triggers won't affect you like they used to. You will begin to have more energy and hope for a beautiful new life. And eventually you will see how life-changing this heroic journey you are on really is, and you will be incredibly proud of yourself for choosing the path of love and life.

CHAPTER TWENTY-FOUR

This is Your Hero's Journey

YOU HAVE BEEN THROUGH AN INCREDIBLY PAINFUL and confusing experience. You have discovered a type of abuse, a form of darkness, you did not know existed. If you experienced the covert type of narcissism, you are one of the pioneers of this knowledge because it is relatively new information in the world of psychology.

The gravity of what you have been through should not be understated. Your physical body has been affected and your heart has been deeply wounded. After what you have been through it would be completely understandable if you felt like shutting out the world. Your trust in people has been affected. Your view of the world has most likely changed. It would be easy for you to feel jaded. It would be tempting to close the door to your heart and live a sheltered life. For a time, you may need to cocoon so you can have space and quiet to heal. We need those times here and there in life.

There are many paths you could take after this type of abuse. Where you go from here is up to you. This is your life, and you get to choose. If you choose to continue to work on your own healing, this path could lead you to incredible transformation and transcendence. The fact that you have read this far in this book tells me this will be your story.

This path of healing is your hero's journey. I call it this because in the mythology of the hero's journey a person goes through an extraordinary experience, learns a lesson (or two or three or four), wins a victory with that newfound knowledge, then returns home transformed.

You have just won a victory because you have discovered something unknown to most of the world, and you have done something about it. My guess is you have already left or cut off contact with a narcissist in your life, or are in the process of deciding what you need and want to do. Maybe you have children with a narcissist, so you are navigating the healthiest possible road for you and your kids. These are victory steps. You are listening to your wise heart and your intelligent mind and honoring its guidance.

There will be many more victories along the way. Your path to freedom and peace is just beginning. You are taking charge like never before and I am incredibly proud of you because I know the strength and courage that takes.

The final leg of the hero's journey is all about returning home. Deep down inside you, beneath the layers of wounding, is profound peace. The path of healing you are on will bring you back home to the soul within you that knows the truth about love, the truth of who you are, the truth of your worth, and the truth of your magnificence.

To get there, first there is programming to unwind and dissolve. There is truth to discover. Then there is the mending of your heart and the rebuilding of your life, and ultimately the relearning of who you are. This takes love and time.

What becomes so heroic with this journey is that the depth of healing you can achieve reaches even beyond what you have experienced from narcissistic abuse. When we heal these wounds, the pain we've felt from other sources we've experienced in life also joins in the healing. Overlapping wounds and messages are healed together.

Many people are profoundly fearful of letting themselves feel all that is inside them, facing their wounds, sitting with themselves, and allowing their emotions to surface. Most people run from this. This is also why I refer to this as your hero's journey. Deep healing that includes this level of honesty and vulnerability is brave and heroic. Can you imagine if every person on Earth did this? If each person took the time to be with their feelings and to love themselves there? This world would be a different place. This is life-changing work. Not many have the courage and discipline to go down this path. The fact that you are pursuing your own healing tells me you are a strong and special person.

Every time you allow yourself to feel, every time you seek answers, every time you love yourself, every time you go to places that are emotionally uncomfortable, please let yourself know how incredible you are.

You made it through an extraordinary experience. You have learned and are learning so much. You have won victories and will win many more. And you are now returning home to the truth of your magnificent self. You are a gift and a treasure. I am so proud of you, and I am rooting for you every step of the way.

CHAPTER TWENTY-FIVE

Designing Your New Life

*"Don't ask what the world needs. Ask what makes you
come alive and go do it. Because what the world needs is
people who have come alive."*
– HOWARD THURMAN

YOU ARE THE WRITER AND DIRECTOR OF YOUR LIFE. You are the painter, the songwriter, and the visionary. You are the captain of your ship, and nothing and no one knows how to steer your life better than you.

You are also the main character in this story of your beautiful life. For far too long your time and energy have been drained by others who have told you who you are and how you should live your life. It is now time for you to take the reins and create a glorious life for yourself.

One of my favorite movie quotes is from a character named Arthur in the movie, *The Holiday*. He is an older man who has been in the film business since he was a teenager. He is at a restaurant with Iris, played by Kate Winslet, a woman who has been draining herself, hoping a toxic man from her work will love her. Arthur says to her, "Iris, in the movies we have leading ladies, and we have the best friend. You, I can tell, are a leading lady, but for some reason, you're behaving like the best friend." Iris's eyes open up and she replies, "You're so right! You are supposed to be the leading lady of your own life, for God's sakes!"

Imagine your life is a movie. So, leading lady, or leading gentleman, since you are the main character, the protagonist, the one the audience is rooting for and wants to see overcome all your obstacles and have a happy ending, where do you want your story to go from here? What has happened so far is only part of your story. There is so much more left to tell. So, as the writer and director, what do you want to see happen for you, the main character in this important story?

If you could decide how the rest of your life is going to play out, what would it look like? Allow yourself to dream here. What would your ideal home be like? When you open your closet what do you see? Flip-flops? Boots? Coats? Summer dresses? Cozy sweaters? When you walk outside, what scenery are you looking at? The ocean? Mountains? A lanai? A large open field? Rolling hills? A bustling downtown?

What would your ideal relationships be like? Are you with someone you love? If you are, how do they treat you? How do you feel around them? Remember, this is your dream, no one else's. Everything in it must feel good to you. You don't have to worry about how to make this happen. For now, just allow yourself to dream. Give yourself permission to let your heart soar as you open to what would feel wonderful.

What kinds of things do you see yourself doing in your ideal life?

Below is space for you to write down anything that comes to you. Write away, dear adventurer. Paint that canvas. I'll get the popcorn. I can't wait to see what you create. Where would you like your story to go from here?

If you are not clear on this right now, that's okay. Give it time. Come back to it when ideas come. Let this be playful. If at any point it feels like work, take a break and come back to it when it feels fun again.

CHAPTER TWENTY-SIX

A Love Letter

Dear Reader,

You have been through a tremendous amount. None of what you experienced was your fault. You are a beautiful person, and you deserve so much better.

It will take time to heal the wounds. Be gentle with yourself. Be kind. Be compassionate. Take things slowly.

Give yourself grace. No judgment. No blame. Just grace.

With time, love, and self-care, your heart will heal. Your energy will return.

Please know you are perfect just the way you are. There is nothing that needs to change in you for you to be worthy of love.

You are worthy of love.

You are worthy of respect.

You are worthy of kindness.

You are worthy of a life that is filled with joy.

You deserve to have people in your life who truly love you.

You get to choose who has the privilege of being close to you.

You get to create a life you really want. And you have everything it takes to do that.

If your future self could talk to you now, I am convinced this is what you would hear, "Well done. I am so proud of you. You won't believe what's coming. Keep healing. Keep hope alive. Keep loving yourself. Keep following your dreams. Keep believing in your own capabilities, and in the love that exists in life. It will all be worth it. You'll see."

I am so proud of you for pursuing your own healing. I am so proud of you and impressed with you for surviving. I am in your corner and always will be.

May the rest of your life be filled with everything your heart longs for. You deserve to be happy. You deserve to feel peace. And you deserve to be loved.

With love,

Debbie

Resources

The resources for healing listed below can be found on Debbie Mirza's website, www.debbiemirza.com:

Guided Meditations for Healing After Narcissistic Abuse:

- Self-Love Affirmations
- Bringing Calm to the Nervous System: *Connecting with Your Body and Environment to Help Regulate the Autonomic Nervous System.*
- Rewriting False Messages Received from Narcissists and Toxic People
- 7-Minute Calming and Centering Meditation
- Healing from Relationships Through Hooponopono

Online Courses:

- How to Parent When your Ex is a Covert Narcissist
- 6-Week Healing and Clarity after Narcissistic Abuse
- How to Facilitate a Support Group for Survivors of Narcissistic Abuse

Debbie's Other Books:

- *The Covert Passive Aggressive Narcissist: Recognizing the Traits and Finding Healing After Hidden Emotional and Psychological Abuse*
- *The Safest Place Possible: A Guide to Healing and Transformation*
- *The Safest Place Possible Companion Book*
- *El Narcisista Pasivo-Agresivo Encubierto: Reconociendo las características y encontrando sanación después del abuso emocional y psicológico oculto*

Debbie's Music to Bring Calm and Encouragement:

- *Soul Rising* album

Recommended Books About Healing Trauma:

- *Healing Trauma* by Peter A. Levine
- *The Body Keeps the Score: Brain, Mind, and Body in the Healing of Trauma* by Bessel van der Kolk M.D.
- *The Heart of Trauma: Healing the Embodied Brain in the Context of Relationships* by Bonnie Badenoch
- *Reclaiming Your Body* by Suzanne Scurlock-Durana

Other Book Recommendations for Healing:

- *The Secret Language of Your Body* by Inna Segal
- *Becoming Supernatural* by Dr. Joe Dispenza
- *The Brain's Way of Healing* by Norman Doidge

ABOUT THE AUTHOR

DEBBIE MIRZA is an author and singer/songwriter. She has a tender and caring heart for people who have experienced narcissistic abuse and has created resources to help survivors heal from this type of trauma. Other books she has written are *The Covert Passive Aggressive Narcissist* and *The Safest Place Possible*. Her book about covert narcissism is also available in Spanish.

Debbie feels honored to be on this path with you and looks forward to writing more books and creating more projects that will help people heal and be able to see the true magnificence of who they really are.

To find out more about Debbie's resources, such as her online support group, online courses, guided meditations, her calming and encouraging music, her other books, and more, go to www.debbiemirza.com.